Veteran Educators, International Education, and Study Abroad

Perspectives, Insights, and Practices

Editors

Thomas V. Millington
Krishna Bista
Roy Y. Chan
Bo Zhang

STAR Scholars Press

First Published 2024

by
STAR Scholars Press
Baltimore, Maryland (US)

Category
Education/Higher Education

Series
Comparative and International Education

Editors
Thomas V. Millington | Krishna Bista | Roy Y. Chan | Bo Zhang

ISBN: 978-1-957480-29-9

Library of Congress Control Number: 2021943754
Veteran Educators, International Education, and Study Abroad: Perspectives, Insights, and Practices
Subject: Education/Higher Education – United States | International Education | Student Mobility | Comparative Education

Library of Congress
US Programs, Law, and Literature Division
Cataloging in Publication Program
101 Independence Avenue, S.E.
Washington, DC 20540-4283

Printed in the United States of America
Typeset: Guru Mantra
Cover Design: Sahar Aghasafari

press.starscholars.org

Veteran Educators, International Education, and Study Abroad

Perspectives, Insights, and Practices

This book offers profound insights into the dynamic landscape of international education, drawing on the perspectives of veteran educators and thought leaders. Through engaging chapters, it explores the transformative potential of global learning, examining current challenges, reflecting on historical trajectories, and envisioning the future of education abroad. Each chapter seamlessly integrates personal experiences, theoretical frameworks, and historical perspectives, emphasizing the vital role of Senior International Officers and advocating for a quantum approach to education abroad. The book aims to deliver a comprehensive and authentic exploration of international education by covering the evolution of study abroad, evolving narratives, and the impacts of political shifts and technology. Beyond celebrating achievements, it addresses critical areas requiring attention, inviting readers on a reflective journey to appreciate the intricate threads forming the tapestry of global education.

Editors
Thomas V. Millington is the Founder and Executive Director of Abroadia, New York, USA. Email: tom@abroadia.com
Krishna Bista is a Professor of Higher Education at Morgan State University, Maryland, USA. Email: krishna.bista@morgan.edu
Roy Y. Chan is an Assistant Professor of Education and Ed.D. Program Director at Lee University, Tennessee, USA. Email: rchan@leeuniversity.edu
Bo Zhang is a TESOL instructor and district administrator at Providence Public Schools in Rhode Island who recently earned a doctoral degree from the University of Hartford, Connecticut, USA. Email: bzhang@hartford.edu

New Titles

1. *Rethinking Hybrid and Remote Work in Higher Education: Global Perspectives, Policies, and Practices after COVID-19*
2. *Online Teaching and Learning in Asian Higher Education*
3. *Unintended Consequences of Internationalization in Higher Education*
4. *Chinese Students and the Experience of International Doctoral Study in STEM*
5. *International Students from Asia in Canadian Universities*
6. *Transforming Lives at the Institutional Level: Equity Promotion Initiatives Across the World*
7. *Making Learning Happen: Five Shifts Toward Student-Focused Education*
8. *Curriculum Theory and Pedagogy for Student Mobility: Research and Practice in International Higher Education*
9. *Advancing Socially Driven Scholarship*
10. *International Graduate and Doctoral Student Experience: Navigating Relationships, Resources, and Resilience*
11. *International Student Identities and Mental Well-Being*
12. *Faculty Engagement and Internationalization at Home in Iceland*
13. *International Student Employability: Narratives of Strengths, Challenges, and Strategies from Global South Students*
14. *Institutional Commitment to Global Engagement*
15. *Cross-Cultural Narratives: Real Stories and Lived Experiences of Global Scholars*
16. *Shaping a Humane World Through Global Higher Education: Pre-Challenges and Post-Opportunities During a Pandemic*
17. *Developing Intercultural Competence in Higher Education*
18. *Global Footprints in Higher Education*
19. *Home and Abroad: International Student Experiences and Graduate Employability*
20. *Global Higher Education During COVID-19: Policy, Society, and Technology*

https://press.starscholars.org/

Contents

Praise for this book

Veteran Educators, International Education, and Study Abroad: Perspectives, Insights, and Practices

"The volume has assembled a distinguished roster of education abroad scholar-practitioners who provide a candid retrospective on the twists and turns of education abroad programming and practice over the past decades. The authors discuss the challenges and successes in education abroad, tracing its journey from the days when there was minimal support to today's thriving profession and robust field. The book offers a rich tapestry of experiences, lessons, and recommendations for those passionate about the future of international learning and engagement."

Anthony C. Ogden, Founder and Managing Director of Gateway International Group. A respected scholar-practitioner with nearly 30 years of experience in international higher education, he has held senior international leadership positions at Pennsylvania State University, the University of Kentucky, Michigan State University, and the University of Wyoming. He is co-editor of *Education Abroad: Bridging Scholarship and Practice* (Routledge, 2021).

"Authentic, captivating, and insightful!!! The lived experiences within these pages seamlessly navigate the complexities of crossing borders, global learning, and cultural understanding. Harnessing the influence of international education, the authors embrace the unfamiliar as liberatory and empowering. This book is an informative and inspiring read that is undoubtedly ideal for students, practitioners, and academics."

Kayon Morgan, Ph.D., is an Assistant Professor at the University of Hartford, USA. Affiliations: American Educational Research Association (AERA) and the British Educational Leadership, Management & Administration Society (BELMAS). Author of *Needing to Be Seen, Longing to Be Heard: Empowering*

Educators of Color through Affinity Groups (IGI Global, 2023) and *Towards a Framework of Parental Involvement and Family Engagement in Jamaica: A Systematic Review* (UWI Press, 2022).

"A compelling and thought-provoking read, this book skillfully weaves personal experiences with a deep understanding of the global education landscape. It underscores the crucial role of Senior International Officers while shedding light on the multifaceted challenges and opportunities shaping study abroad today. A must-read for anyone passionate about international education."

'Dimeji R. Togunde, Ph.D. is Professor of International Studies and Vice Provost for Global Education at Spelman College, USA. A respected scholar-practitioner, he is a co-editor of *Institutional Commitment to Global Engagement: Cross-Cultural Reflections of Faculty, Students, Staff, and Alumnae at Spelman College* (STARS Scholar Press, 2023) and has contributed chapters to several books, including "*The Half Yet To Be Told: Study Abroad and HBCUs* (The Forum on Study Abroad, 2023); *"Reimagining Internationalization and International Initiatives at Historically Black Colleges and Universities"* (Palgrave Macmillan 2022).

Acknowledgments

This book would not have been possible without the support, knowledge, and guidance of the team at the STAR Scholars Network. In particular, we wish to recognize Dr. Uttam Gaulee, and Dr. Roy Y. Chan for their time and support in this project. Many people work behind the scenes to bring about a successful publication and we acknowledge their fundamental role in pushing this project through its completion.

This book was created to address a need identified by the STAR Scholars Network and to assess the historiography of international education through its many manifestations, development, and growth.

We are grateful to the Humane Letters Grants for making this project successful.

We give special thanks to all the authors who contributed significantly to this book. Quite simply, without their effort, this book would not have been published.

Introduction

"To live past the end of your myth is a perilous thing."
-Anne Carson

"The virtue and rightness of a cause are not alone the condition and cause of its acceptance."
-A. Philip Randolph

When one mentions "international education" it invokes images of a noble profession, one that makes a valuable contribution, whatever that may be, to making the world a better place. On college and university campuses it oscillates between the spheres of academics, student services, and career services. For some in the profession, it has become a repository for "enthusiastic gush," while for others, it is a collective of "self-proclaimed experts free to make their own calls." The outcomes of international education are sometimes subverted to its aspirations. The intangibles of international education, i.e., learning a second language, dealing with ambiguity, becoming a global citizen, etc., are deftly used by marketing specialists, both within higher education and without, to recruit students. But have we ever stopped to consider how "achievable" international education is? The Holocaust historian Piotr Cywinski is critical of the construction of a "united" world. He states that "I don't believe in something like, 'the conscience of the world'. There are over seven billion consciences in the world. We must reach real human beings, not some mythical sum, to do some good" (Simon, 2020). With Mr. Cywinski's statement in mind, this book intends to offer a survey of the international education landscape by reviewing the challenges it has faced in years past and exploring what the future may hold for it. The authors have investigated international education beyond the "mythical sum" it aspires to. During this examination, international educators will challenge and scrutinize the "idea," the "identity," and "goals" of international education, with the hope that through their efforts we may establish a clearer path forward for the field. The authors will probe the essence of international education to discover what makes the field so special to its practitioners. How has it changed over the last 50 years? Does it have a historiography? Can it provide students with the skills needed for employment after graduation? Does it prioritize one body of knowledge over another? Is it acyclic (that is, will its trajectory return to its beginnings as a vehicle for second-language acquisition, or will it continue to march forward through new and uncharted territory)?

The novelist Salman Rushdie wrote, "The birth of a great idea revealed things about its future, the way in which newness enters the world prophesied how it would behave when it grew old" (Rushdie, 2012, p. 45). The concept of "international education" has been with us for years, but there has never been an immutable Weltanschauung that provided an anchor upon which international education could base its identity. In its earliest conception, international education was deemed to be essential to learning a second language; then it became a prominent form of citizen diplomacy; later it was extolled as a wonderful way to create a global workforce and now it is being tasked to serve as a moral entrepreneur to combat racism. How permanent are these values? The Scottish philosopher William MacAskill has written about "early plasticity, later rigidity" where he posits that "it can be much easier to influence the norms, standards and laws surrounding a technology, idea or country when they are still new than later on when things have settled" (MacAskill, 2022, p. 79). In many ways, international education is still in an epoch of plasticity, incorporating new trends, ideas, and philosophies in its vision paralleling the prevalent concepts and strategic thinking of the years. It struggles to make its way forward through a miasma of good intentions. For the moment, it lacks what MacAskill calls a "value lock-in...an event that causes a single value system or set of value systems to persist for an extremely long time." What are the values that we hope international education will lock in?

Leading thought leaders in international education and other disciplines have made astute observations about underlying trends and developments in the field. Could these trends and developments become the field's lock-in values? Bryan McAllister-Grande, founder and director of GlobalEd, cites the need for a shift toward "epistemic plurality", where there are, "More diversity of thought and perspectives beyond what remains largely mobility-focused definitions (despite the recent leap in thinking.)". Wei/David Liu, PhD, from the University of Alberta International, critically notes that in too many cases university pursuit of new sources of funding eclipses the goals of higher international education. He writes, "In a highly neoliberal environment, the higher education internationalization efforts in the Global North have focused overwhelmingly on generating revenue through international recruitment, with an insufficient consideration of universities' role in contributing to world equality and sustainability."

Liz Bucar, professor of religion and Dean's Leadership Fellow at Northeastern University, warns us about the potential ethical quagmire that education abroad programs can become by unwittingly promoting "epistemic injustice" through their misperception of cultural immersion, cultural appropriation, false advertising and incomplete historical representations of the oppressed in the host countries (Bucar, 2023). Should we consider the international education collectivity a "community" (a body of individuals who have in common a method of deciding disputes) or a "group" (a social gathering which lacks a decision procedure)? The philosopher Virginia Held asks whether a group of individuals can be morally responsible (Held, 1991, pp. 265-288). Before answering that question international education must reconcile the conflicting minutiae of its moral entrepreneurship. For example, under its global citizenship guise, it claims to foster better relations between people of diverse cultures and nations via soft skills such as diplomacy, cross-cultural empathy, and engagement. Yet, as the field stakes a claim to promote anti-racism, it has not adequately pondered or digested perspectives that may challenge its diplomatic or global citizenship ethos. Myisha Cherry (2022, p.12) presents the case for using Lourdean rage as an effective activist tool. She calls for an "image variation view" which "appreciates the varieties and complexity that anger contains." In order to be a more effective tool for global citizenship and anti-racism, international education must synthesize the nuances of both concepts into language that can be fully understood and advocated by individuals in the field (International education has a track record of advocating for moral, ethical, and global standards. In 1963 fifty-nine students from Columbia University defied the Kennedy Administration's travel restrictions against engagement with Cuba by traveling to that country from Prague. More recently, Brethren Colleges Abroad's Dr. James Skelly challenged former Secretary of State Colin Powell during a question-and-answer session at the 2006 Annual NAFSA conference in Minnesota about his view regarding the US invasion of Iraq. For me, these two examples illustrate the power of international education).

While we cannot address the plasticity or rigidity of international education here, nor the value lock-ins we hope it will establish, we can consult those who have served the profession the longest for their perspectives and experience. We can learn from them what the most pressing challenges to the field were when they entered the profession, what they are today, and where they see international education going over the next ten years.

As the world and international educators emerge from the pandemic and navigate a much different landscape than they had encountered previously, many organizations, ed tech companies, think tanks, and analysts have tried to assess the nuances and challenges facing international education. What should be front and center among these examinations is the input from veteran thought leaders in international education. It would be immensely beneficial to the profession, those new to it, and those in higher education who are not acquainted with international education, to become familiar with the perspectives of international educators over the years as they have seen the field grow, flourish, and overcome the many challenges that it has faced.

The philosopher Michael Gelven remarked "History tells a story. Indeed, without the fundamental structure of a story, there would be no history at all, there would only be rude chronology" (Gelven, 1994, p. 57). We asked the contributors to this book to submit chapters to the story that is international education. As the field continues to grow and transform and as future international educators and scholar-practitioners make their mark on international education, we hope that this book will serve as an invaluable tool to help us examine this profession, reflect on it, and appreciate the narrative that is still being written.

References

Bucar, L. (2023, May 19), *Avoiding curricular pratfalls of study abroad*. Inside Higher Education. https://www.insidehighered.com/opinion/views/2023/05/19/avoiding-curricular-pitfalls-study-abroad

Cherry, M. (2022). *The case for rage: Why anger is essential to anti-racist struggle*. Oxford University Press.

Gelven, M. (1994). *War and existence: A philosophical inquiry*. The Pennsylvania State University Press.

Held, V. (1991). Can a random collection of individuals be morally responsible? In P. French (Ed.), *The spectrum of responsibility*. St. Martin's Press.

MacAskill, W. (2022). *What we owe the future*. Basic Books.

Rushdie. S. (2012). *Joseph Anton: A memoir*. Random House.

Simon, S. (2020). *Opinion: Holocaust historian offers to serve 10-year sentence of Nigerian boy*. NPR. Opinion: Holocaust Historian Offers To Serve 10-Year Sentence Of Nigerian Boy: NPR

Chapter 1

A Challenging, But Rewarding Road

Reflecting on the Past, Present and Future of Study Abroad

Gary Rhodes, Ph.D.
Professor and Chair of the Graduate Education Division, College of Education
California State University at Dominguez Hills (CSUDH), United States

Lisa Loberg, Ed.D.
Associate Director of Exchange and Study Away
Art Center College of Design in Southern California, United States

ABSTRACT

This chapter provides a retrospective examination of international education and how Study Abroad in particular has developed and changed over the past 30 years. Study Abroad has gone from having very little administrative or budgetary support to featuring prominently in college mission statements and admission brochures. A body of growing research now supports its beneficial outcomes and contributions to the college experience and beyond. Included in this chapter is a summary of its past, current and future challenges and suggestions of ways enhanced Study Abroad programming might look in the future, including greater connection to the Olympic Movement, University International Athletics, and the United Nations Sustainable Development Goals. Above all, the authors contend that Study Abroad should be enhanced, supported and celebrated, as it continues to be an important educational tool in fostering international peace and cross-cultural understanding.

Keywords: Education Abroad, International Education, Study Abroad, U.S. Student Mobility, U.N. Sustainable Development Goals, UN SDGs, Olympic Movement, Olympism, University International Athletics

INTRODUCTION

International education has had an interesting evolution at U.S. colleges and universities. There has been a significant amount of growth in the number of programs and in the number of students studying abroad since the authors started working in the field in 1989 (Rhodes) and 2000 (Loberg). This chapter will provide a reflection on the years since, focusing on several levers of change, and conclude by highlighting the potential to enhance the impact of study abroad in the future, using concepts from published resources and personal reflections, along with a dedication to all those who made an impact on the field in the past, in the present, and who will in the future. For a more comprehensive review of the early years of study abroad and the movement forward of the field, the authors suggest *History of U.S. Study Abroad: Beginnings to 1965* (Hoffa, 2007) and *History of U.S. Study Abroad: 1965 – Present* (Hoffa & DePaul, 2010), in addition to the many other publications that provide additional information about the past, present, and future of international education. While international education includes inbound and outbound student mobility, this chapter will focus primarily on the sending of U.S. college and university students abroad, most commonly known as Study Abroad, but also known as Learning Abroad, Study Away, Global Programs, or Education Abroad, to name a few variations.

Student Participation and the Importance of Study Abroad

Participation in study abroad by U.S. undergraduate students has increased steadily over the past three decades: from just 70,727 students in 1989/90, to over 100,000 (113,959) for the first time in the 1997/98 academic year, to over 200,000 (205,983) for the first time in 2004/05, to over 300,000 (304,467) for the first time in 2013/14, hitting a high of 347,099 in 2018/19, before the reduction in participation resulting from COVID-19 to 14,549 in 2020/21 (Institute of International Education, 2022). These increases have been accompanied by the upsurge in 2- and 4-year college enrollment: from 11.9 million in 1990 to 16.5 million in 2019 (NCES, 2021). The overall percentage of students enrolled in college who studied abroad in a given year was just .05% in 1990 and remained relatively low at 2.1% in 2019.

For the students who participated, the importance of study abroad in the 1990s and early 2000s was often focused on general ideas of learning a language other than English and about curricular content areas with an international focus, as well as the personal desire to explore the world outside of the U.S. The movement forward from the World Wars continued to also highlight the importance of study abroad to support international understanding and peace, as indicated by the often-cited statement by William Fulbright, and to limit the potential of another world war:

Education is a slow-moving but powerful force. It may not be fast enough or strong enough to save us from catastrophe, but it is the strongest force available for that purpose, and in its proper place, therefore, is not at the periphery, but at the center of international relations. We should consider trans-national educational exchange not solely or even primarily as an intellectual or academic experience, but as the most effective means (in the words of Albert Einstein) "to deliver mankind from the menace of war (Fulbright, p. 29).

Carlson and Widaman (1988) found that a junior year abroad contributed to increased levels of international political concern and cross-cultural interest among college student participants, and it positively impacted their attitudes towards other cultures (p. 13). Many who supported study abroad, from higher education leaders to program faculty and administrators, highlighted the potential for study abroad to make an impact on the relationships of people around the world; however, there was really no field-wide training for faculty or staff on how to design study abroad programs to directly impact international relations and peace or to implement pre-departure, while-abroad or re-entry training to support that impact. Follow-up surveys after study abroad did not regularly provide valid and reliable quantitative or qualitative data to identify the impact of study abroad to support improved international relations and peace. The primary re-entry surveys asked students practical questions about their courses, their housing, and their excursions while abroad. Most colleges and universities did not look deeply at other impacts, including international relations and peace; curriculum integration; the impact of study abroad on retention and success toward degrees; or career and professional development. Formal research and analysis focused on these potential positive outcomes of study abroad would come about much later.

The Emergence of Study Abroad Offices

In the 1990s, comprehensively staffed study abroad offices were few and far between. If there was support around outbound mobility, for many institutions it was in the form of a one-person office, or a lone faculty member tasked with signing approval forms and helping students find their way abroad and back. The level of staffing and resources at colleges and universities with a study abroad office rarely included a staff member responsible for safety and crisis management or focused on diversity, equity, and inclusion. Often, the study abroad office was fairly isolated on campus, its structure usually on the academic side of the house and not set up to engage formally with offices on campus whose role was to effectively lead and manage university programs, or with comprehensive support and expertise related to student affairs and services issues.

Leaders and staff in a study abroad office often fell into those positions by chance. It may have been a faculty member who had studied abroad themselves, immigrated to the United States, or had an international background. Staff members may have been moved into the study abroad office with no formal background or experience in international education. Faculty leaders may have had a master's or doctoral degree, but not from an academic degree area focused on internationalization of higher education administration. Many staff members at the time may have had a bachelor's degree, but often no formal training on study abroad program development, administration, or student support. When Rhodes entered the field, NAFSA's Section on U.S. Students Abroad (SECUSSA, now the Education Abroad Knowledge Community) offered a very basic pre-conference workshop during the NAFSA Annual Conference, titled: *Study Abroad 101*.

Academic training for professionals and research to support their work in the field was limited. Graduate degrees in international and intercultural education were focused primarily on international development in developing countries, with minimal if any focus on the internationalization of higher education or study abroad. Graduate degrees in higher education focused on university management and student affairs administration; they paid very little attention to study abroad as a sub-area needing specialized teaching/learning and research. Some research and research-based publications focused on content related to language or cross-cultural learning; research on study abroad was less prolific and remained largely out of sight.

Administrative and Academic Changes and the "Year of Study Abroad"

In 1987, even before the development of a common currency in Europe, the "Erasmus" program was created to facilitate student mobility between European institutions. During the first 30 years of the program, from 1987 – 2017, over nine million students received support to study, train, volunteer or gain professional experience abroad (European Commission, 2017, para. 3).

This level of coordinated support or infrastructure did not exist in the U.S. in the 1990s. In late 2005, by unanimous vote, the U.S. Senate declared 2006 the "Year of Study Abroad," recognizing that "educating students internationally is an important way to share the values of the United States, to create goodwill for the United States around the world, to work toward a peaceful global society, and to increase international trade" (Res. 308, p. 1). U.S. Senator Richard Durbin wrote of his support for international education and commended the development of the Lincoln Commission, which intended to increase participation in study abroad; Senator Durbin looked ahead with optimism to the "future of study abroad" (2006, p. 4).

The national spotlight was helpful, and it added visibility and lent credibility to campus proposals for the expansion of international study opportunities and the creation of study abroad offices. Language about the importance of global perspectives began to appear in university mission statements, and global engagement efforts became a regular mention in the speeches of college presidents. While international students were already seen as an important source of revenue at many college and university campuses, sending students abroad had often been viewed as a loss of tuition revenue, particularly for smaller, tuition-dependent institutions. Advocacy and data began to change this viewpoint around study abroad. For many campuses, a capacity building phase for study abroad involves cross-functional collaboration with various administrative offices on campus to create the necessary infrastructure with student services, billing, transfer of credit, financial aid, and other areas of support.

Perceptions also began to shift favorably when study abroad was among "High-Impact Activities" Kuh identified as "unusually effective" (2008, p. 14-21). Sutton and Rubin began looking at how studying abroad affects factors such as retention and graduation rates (2004, p. 76). A majority of prospective college students indicated interest in studying abroad during college (American Council on Education and Art & Science, 2008, p. 3), which was of interest to admission officers. The link between a study abroad experience, transferable skills, and career preparation was beginning to be part of the conversation, as well (Hubbard & Rexeisen, 2020, pp. 4-5).

Institutional agreements, exchange partnerships, and MOUs (Memoranda of Understanding) became more prolific, as instant methods of written communication made the world a smaller place. More study abroad provider organizations arrived on the scene to accommodate growing student interest and to meet increased demand for on-site support (Faupel, 2017, pp. 96-97). Growth in participation in study abroad programs and the increased access to non-traditional destinations can, in part, be attributed to the efforts of third-party providers which organize academic opportunities abroad that can include students on a grouped program in many countries and cities around the world from many different U.S. colleges and universities. This is particularly important for providing programs for a student, when their home campus does not have enough students to host a program with just their own students.

Participation in study abroad overall has increased, but the definition of a study abroad program has also expanded, termed by some as "education abroad." Along with traditional university courses, there are also other international experiential learning opportunities, including internships, field study, volunteering, teaching, and conducting research abroad. The concept of the "Junior Year Abroad" often with a heavy emphasis on language learning has transitioned to programs of various models and lengths of time. Dwyer (2004) found that more time in-country was indeed beneficial (pp. 155-156) across factors that are "strongly embraced by study abroad professionals" (p. 152). However, student participation in year-long study abroad has remained relatively flat or decreased over time. The real growth in study abroad participation has been with semester-long and shorter-term programs, which may occur during a semester, during a winter or spring break and during the summer months. These types of programs have made international study experiences accessible to more students, including students at community colleges (Raby & Rhodes, 2018), athletes, and students with family responsibilities.

The professionalization of international education has also flourished. Graduate degree programs focused on international educational administration are now more widely available and are producing researchers and leaders. Several professional organizations now exist to support those who work in the study abroad field. NAFSA, which is celebrating 75 years as a professional organization, was originally the "National Association of Foreign Student Advisers". By 1990, it had already been renamed to include a broader range of areas of emphasis: "NAFSA: Association of International Educators." While NAFSA provided resources that were mostly U.S.-focused, for both inbound and outbound student mobility, some study abroad professionals felt that NAFSA did not provide enough emphasis on or support for outbound. study abroad. They formed a new organization in 2001: The Forum on Education Abroad. "The Forum" was designated as a standards development organization for the field and continues its unique focus on outbound study abroad. There has also been the growth of international education organizations that support student mobility in other regions of the world, including: the European Association of International Education, Asia Pacific Association for International Education, International Education Association for New Zealand and Australia, and the

International Education Association of South Africa, along with other regional and country-specific international higher education organizations.

Finally, it is prudent to recognize the impact of technology on the study abroad office. The internet provided a significant change in communication and information sharing for the study abroad field (Rhodes, 1995). Advances in technology paved the way for transitioning from paper applications to electronic databases. Paper catalogs have been replaced with digital versions. In addition to these office efficiencies, we want to highlight the advances that resulted in the ability to instantly communicate with colleagues around the world. The first Apple Macintosh computer was released in 1984, and it was not long ago that the first iPhone was released in 2007. Before the regular use of computers, cell phones, and the internet, communication was by phone, fax, or mail, and long-distance international calls were expensive. Before study abroad search engines were widely available, the Institute of International Education (IIE) publication: *IIE Passport* and *Peterson's Guides* provided printed reference directories of available study abroad programs—they were basically huge reference books of available study abroad programs. The speed at which we can now communicate is truly remarkable, and with the regular use of cell phones, texting, social media, Zoom meetings and video calls, technological communication methods have helped to overcome some of the challenges of working with programs around the world.

CURRENT CHALLENGES

Ensuring Access to Study Abroad

While study abroad programming continues to grow in its popularity and in its sophistication, many students have been left out when it comes to participation (Lopez-McGee Comp & Contreras, 2018; Netz et al., 2020). Much more needs to be done in the areas of equity, diversity, and inclusion to ensure greater access to study abroad opportunities among students who have been historically underrepresented. Many variables can positively or negatively impact a student's intent to study abroad, including background, academic major, distance of university from home (Stroud, 2010). Other factors include the ways in which program opportunities are marketed (Boulden, 2022), the kinds of support structures in place for student identities, administrative barriers, and the perception of cost, which can all impact a student's decision to apply or not, or to ultimately participate or not.

NAFSA has had a special interest group focused on increasing diversity in study abroad,while the Forum on Education Abroad has developed resources and support in this area, and additional resources, support, and visibility around these issues have also increased. Diversity Abroad, an organization founded in 2006 with a mission "to create equitable access to the benefits of global education by empowering educators, engaging stakeholders, and connecting diverse students to resources and opportunity" has also made an important impact.

There is growing awareness around supporting students with disabilities and the need for accommodations that help ensure that all students in higher education have a path to participation. The U.S. Department of State has provided funding to Mobility International USA to create additional resources and programs to increase study abroad opportunities for students with special needs and disabilities. *IIE Open Doors* now includes a section on participation data focused on "Students with Disability."

Cost and the perception of cost continue to prevent more students from studying abroad. While there are few specialized scholarships for low-income and middle-income families, the U.S. Department of State's Benjamin A. Gilman International Scholarship Program (targeted to "Pell-eligible", students with high financial need, over the past 20 years, has provided support for students with high financial need to study abroad. According to Valuy and Shao (2021), "Gilman Scholars represent the full diversity of the United States and a vast expansion of opportunities for students who have been traditionally underrepresented in study abroad" (p. 14). Colleges and universities must expand upon these efforts to ensure that all students have a financial path to study abroad.

Health and Safety

With the expansion of programs and increased student participation, overseas incidents involving health, safety, security, and mental health are leading to an increased focus on emergency response, preparation, institutional risk management, and the development of more campus-wide policies and procedures. The management of these incidents is often added to the responsibilities of international educators, who already wear many hats in the course of their work (Rhodes et al., 2013). The Overseas Security Advisory Council (OSAC) in the U.S. Department of State has provided support and increased governmental health and safety resources for college and university study abroad faculty and staff since the 1990s. In the early 1990s, there were few full-time staff focused on health and safety or crisis and risk management for study abroad.

Highly publicized incidents of student death and injury during a study abroad experience resulted in a formal response from the field in the development of the 1998 document *Responsible Study Abroad: Health and Safety Guidelines* (NAFSA, 1998). The Fund for the Improvement of Post-Secondary Education (FIPSE) of the U.S. Department of Education provided a Comprehensive Program Grant in 1998 to support the development of health and safety resources through the SAFETI Clearinghouse at the Center for Global Education at the University of Southern California. The Center for Global Education later moved to Loyola Marymount University in 2004, to UCLA in 2010, and to California State University at Dominguez Hills in 2015. The health and safety "guidelines" of 1998 had been revised in the *Interorganizational Task Force on Safety and Responsibility in Study Abroad* (NAFSA, 2002) and became "best practices" when The Forum on Education Abroad and NAFSA convened the *Joint Task Force on Health, Safety, and Security* (2021). Many colleges, universities, and study abroad organizations have now put in place full-time staff focused on supporting institutional health, safety, crisis and risk management. The organization PULSE International was created in 2010 to support staff whose focus is study abroad health and safety (Pulse International, 2022).

While there has been an increase in staff and resources dedicated to health, safety, crisis management and security, there is still a differentiation between institutions with comprehensive study abroad offices and resources, and community colleges and universities with no full-time study abroad staff and very limited resources, which in turn limits opportunities and effective support for study abroad.

Navigating a Global Pandemic

Due to the COVID-19, in just the past three years, almost all international education professionals have had to face closing down all their study abroad programs in a way that had previously only existed in table-top exercises. The scenario of "how to evacuate an entire study abroad program and bring all of your students and faculty home", along with navigating unknowns, responding to changing conditions, rapidly setting policy, and communicating responses to stakeholders, is now on the resumes of most international education staff, following the onset of the global pandemic beginning in spring 2020. As the world opened back up after the COVID-19 was under control, decisions had to be made around restarting programs and were based on up-to-the-minute information about local laws and informed by campus and higher education community expectations. Study abroad offices parallel many of the complex responsibilities of running a university, with the added layer of implementing academic programs in a global setting (Rhodes et al, 2013). Study Abroad offices that are highly resourced have been able to support the regrowth of study abroad programs more efficiently than would have been possible in the past.

Along with the remote work and virtual learning happening on home campuses, the pandemic brought about opportunities for a virtual study abroad office, allowing students to engage with advisors in a remote setting. Instead of coming to campus for an advising appointment, students were able to connect with staff individually through virtual appointments. Information sessions could be delivered in a virtual format using Zoom meetings. Many campuses have continued to offer both in-person and virtual methods for students to connect with study abroad staff for individual advising and group information sessions.

The pandemic mainstreamed virtual learning for home campuses and created more opportunities for internationally based learning, including courses taught online by faculty abroad and remote internships with overseas organizations. When the COVID-19 pandemic conditions eased, there was immediate interest in returning to in-person programming and travel. Virtual learning, however, does have long-term potential in the international space, including academic programs such as COIL: Collaborative Online International Learning, that facilitate cross-cultural partnerships and academic activities with faculty and students around the world (SUNY, 2023).

While many college and university study abroad offices have grown over the years, the suspension of international programming and travel during COVID-19 resulted in a reduction in funding and staffing for many study abroad offices and private study abroad organizations. In some cases, offices have not yet returned to pre-pandemic staffing or funding levels. At the same time, the numbers of study abroad programs and students studying abroad are returning to the same levels they were before the pandemic at some colleges and universities. These changes and reductions in staffing are putting pressure on colleges, universities and study abroad organizations to provide the same quality of support. The additional pressure on faculty and staff is leading to cases of burnout among study abroad professionals; some have changed institutions and others have left the field of international education entirely to pursue opportunities in other industries.

Even prior to the pandemic, campus offices rarely grew in proportion to the workload or responsibility. It is important that colleges, universities and study abroad providers don't wait for under-supported programs and the resulting weaknesses in program implementation that could also result in a growth in health and safety incidents abroad.

With the return to study abroad growth and changes in staffing, it is even more important for all offices, but in particular, under-resourced offices to collaborate with colleagues across campus to provide adequate support to students. An important area of need for additional resources and support on-campus and for study abroad programs, for example, is the growth in students requiring special mental health support abroad, which can be critical to student success and health and safety. The concept of global academic mobility is certainly not new (Hoffa, 2007), but the expanding landscape in international education, the return to increased participation after the COVID-19 pandemic, events happening around the world, and the proliferation of programs and partnerships, all bring about new challenges and opportunities. If the last few years are any indication, the next decade will offer many more challenges and opportunities for the study abroad field.

Climate Change: Balancing the Cost and Benefit of Travel

International educators are becoming more aware of the carbon footprint of international travel. Balancing the benefits of global mobility with the environmental cost is a challenge, but we also know that an academic experience abroad can have a lifelong impact on civic engagement and advocacy (Paige et al., 2009). Students who study abroad may come away with a greater appreciation for the climate issues in the countries where they study, including the eco-conscious strategies they encounter, such as the availability of public transportation, the use of renewable energy and other eco-friendly practices. International education, with effective program design and effective pre-departure, while abroad, and re-entry learning can be seen as an investment in the future. Providing opportunities for students to plan before going abroad, be intentional while abroad, and reflect on their time abroad after returning home can greatly enhance the impact. Faculty and staff can design intentional learning to help students consider how to make a positive impact now and in the future from what they have learned in and out of the classroom during study abroad as a key to making a positive lifelong impact.

As organizations strive to become carbon neutral by self-imposed deadlines, study abroad offices should be mindful of a similar calculation and offer ways to offset impact with more climate conscious choices. This should include providing students with learning that includes greater environmental awareness. While the focus is often on the carbon footprint of the international flight, understanding the carbon cost of daily life, including food choices and other sustainable practices, represents an important opportunity for meaningful offset and learning.

Study Abroad, Connecting to Other Global Events Supporting International Learning and Understanding, Including the Olympic and Paralympic Games, the International University Sports Federation, and the United Nations Sustainable Development Goals

Study abroad is becoming a more visible part of the higher education experience, yet we know that still only a small percentage of college and university students are studying abroad. Many people in the U.S. are only aware of studying abroad if their friend or family member were studying abroad. Connecting to other organizations that are not part of the traditional higher education study abroad community, but are more popular, may help increase the visibility of study abroad and increase the impact of study abroad programs.

One effort could include growing connections to the Olympic Movement. Every two (2) years, over 25% of the world's population focuses on the Summer or Winter Olympic and Paralympic Games. The Olympic Movement includes the concept of "Olympism", which includes the three values of excellence, respect, and friendship. "They constitute the foundation on which the Olympic Movement builds its activities to promote sport, culture and education with a view to building a better world." (Olympic Museum, 2023). As a part of the value of "Friendship", "the Olympic Movement includes ideals and values of connecting people around the world in ways that increase mutual understanding and peace" (Olympic Museum, 2023). Many U.S. college and university students participate in the Olympic and Paralympic Games. Supporting those students and making the connection between their international athletic experience and study abroad efforts on campus, provides the opportunity to add additional focus on international learning and understanding for these student athletes.

The International University Sports Federation (FISU) also provides an opportunity for U.S. college and university athletic programs to represent their home campus and interact with athletes from colleges and universities outside the U.S. through sports. "FISU organises world-class sports and educational events, all with the mission of providing university students with the opportunities to connect and exchange with students from around the world, in a collaborative and competitive environment (FISU 2023).

To make a significant impact, connecting to internationally recognized goals can help create clear areas where faculty, staff and students can focus learning and design outcomes to make an impact. The United Nations Sustainable

Development Goals (UN SDGs) have been seen as a mechanism to allow students and study abroad organizations to deepen the teaching, learning, and understanding of the impact that can be made through connecting international learning to the UN SDGs. The International Olympic Committee has highlighted the potential of sport to help achieve 11 of the UN SDGs. The United Nations has "sport as a means to promote education, health, development and peace", and highlights the important role of the IOC and the Olympic Movement in achieving these goals (International Olympic Committee, 2023).

FISU has also developed a special connection to the UN SDGs. "The FISU Healthy Campus programme was also developed with the goal of creating an international benchmark for physical health and mental wellbeing on university campuses around the world. This programme is designed to benefit students and staff, while helping implement the United Nations Sustainable Development Goals (FISU, 2023). FISU has developed a way to highlight universities that have become models for supporting the FISU Healthy Campus program. "A 'FISU Healthy Campus Label' will be awarded to acknowledge the universities' efforts in improving the quality of life on their campuses" (FISU, 2021).

The Forum on Education Abroad has also created an "Award for Advancing the UN SDGs Through Education Abroad," which is supported by their content focused on "Advancing the UN Sustainable Development Goals through Education Abroad." This toolkit includes background information, a UN SDG Impact Table, and Workshops on the UN SDGs (Forum on Education Abroad, 2021). Rankings organizations, including Times Higher Education Impact Rankings, the QS World University Rankings focus on the Sustainable Development Goals, and others can provide ways to highlight efforts being made by institutions through study abroad to impact the UN SDGs.

THE STUDY ABROAD WORLD OF THE FUTURE

"*Education is the most powerful weapon you can use to change the world.*" (Nelson Mandela, July 16, 2003).

The challenge for study abroad is to show how it can effectively change the world in positive ways. In this section, the authors intend to provide some areas where the future of study abroad program development and implementation can serve to help make this impact more significant.

The future will certainly include both the challenges and opportunities inherent in the growth of advances in technology and the use of technology in higher education. This will include questions of how language and culture learning on computer and mobile apps might connect with majors and minors and classes at colleges and universities. COVID-19 has increased the use of virtual international learning; future international learning designs can include hybrid opportunities to maximize the impact of both virtual and in-person learning.

Challenges for the future, including those outlined by the United Nations Sustainable Development Goals, as well as conflict within and between countries around the world, highlight the need for greater international and intercultural learning around the world.

Being in a country outside the United States is a meaningful experience for college and university students. Study abroad opportunities can support enhanced skills to communicate, to witness for oneself, to exchange ideas, to understand, and to make a positive impact on oneself and the world. In the next decade, the imperative for international education and study abroad should continue to grow.

What Could Be: The Future Design and Impacts of Study Abroad: Faculty, Staff, Students, and the Community

For Faculty and Staff: Study abroad will continue to grow, integrated with other home campus international learning activities. Resources ideally continue to grow to enable education abroad offices to provide high-impact internationalization at home, with virtual and in-person international learning opportunities with connectivity to faculty and staff in each academic department on campus. Faculty and staff engage in learning also connected to specific colleges and universities outside the U.S. for teaching, research and community service opportunities for individual faculty, staff and students and special programs for academic departments. Student Service offices on campus will engage in broad-ranging support activities with resources to enhance on campus international learning and help support academic and administrative responsibilities connected to international learning. Faculty and staff supporting study abroad will reflect the broad types of diverse groups represented by students, faculty, and staff in higher education. Government agencies and non-profit foundations will increase resources to support program implementation and research. Annual regional, national, and international conferences bring international educators together to share research and ideas, to examine problems and to advance best practices. An increasing number of international educators will continue to obtain graduate degrees and connect research and practice in the field.

For Students: The mobile app that a future college or university student uses during the application process could include an Artificial Intelligence analysis, based on student responses about major, minor, language learning and short-term, medium-term and long-term educational degree goals, which provides them with suggestions for integrating international learning and study abroad as they plan their degree programs. It could also include information about professional development and career interests as well as potential impacts on local and global challenges, with a special focus on responding to the United Nations Sustainable Development Goals. There could be an analysis of the student's academic and career goals, along with potential international dual-degree programs and project partners, which could support international learning with collaborative development projects, a mix of virtual and international learning opportunities, with a number of options for direct course mapping and degree time-line, seamlessly integrating potential study abroad opportunities before, during and after their undergraduate degree program.

Once the student chooses their intended direction, online international learning through virtual and future international education opportunities become available prior to arrival at their college or university campus. Program information will include relevant funding opportunities. Participating students and student workers in study abroad offices will reflect the broad types of diverse groups represented by students, faculty and staff in higher education. Academic content and programs will reflect the interests and needs of students from a broad range of diverse backgrounds.

The planning for international learning integrates the opportunities for students on study abroad to take home campus classes online that are important for two-year completion at a community college and four-year completion for bachelor's degree students, to support students who may require a specific on-campus course being available online, during the semester they when they would be studying outside the United States.

Along with the degree(s) earned at the end of major, minor, language and general education study, students can earn digital badges as they complete efforts before, during and after their internationalization at home and international education/study abroad experience. These digital badges are highlighted and connected to student LinkedIn accounts and other social media platforms. Students who complete international learning at home and abroad are honored when they graduate and graduate schools and companies compete to bring these graduates to their campuses and companies. These graduates continue to be engaged in activities that support international learning and understanding that supports the United Nations Sustainable Development Goals, making a positive impact on the world of the present and future.

For the Broader Community: Through connectivity to the Olympic Movement, the International University Sports Organization (FISU), an increasing number of college and university athletes connect their international competitions to international learning. These athletes as well as the global population that focuses on the Summer and Winter Olympic and Paralympic Games and the colleges and universities who participate in FISU programs also engage more regularly and effectively in support of the United Nations Sustainable Development Goals. Through outreach and educational efforts during the Summer and Winter Olympic and Paralympic Games and other high profile international activities, a greater understanding of opportunities and the importance of international learning as a part of the K-12 and college and university education results in an increasing number of international learning opportunities for students on campus and through study abroad. U.S. colleges and universities increase resources and support and receive recognition and win awards recognizing their support for international education, study abroad, and the UN Sustainable Development Goals.

Dedication to Those Who Came Before, Who Are Working Now, and Future Leaders

We dedicate this article to the students, faculty and staff in the United States and around the world who helped support education/study abroad and the international learning and understanding that came before us; those who are working and doing research in the field now; and who will continue to move the field forward in the future. Since there are so many people who have made an impact for the authors, for the field, and will make an impact in the future, we are including the following blank area, to allow those who read the article to think about those who made an impact for them: ____________________ (consider relevant names for you here). We suggest that you reach out to them to thank them for their efforts.

We believe that we are in a world with opportunities and challenges, and an understanding of the lives and cultures of the many people around the world is critical for responding positively and effectively to the challenges we face; and we believe that education/study abroad with intentional pre-departure, while abroad, and re-entry support, in combination with many other efforts, including support for the UN Sustainable Development Goals, is key to the outcomes that help make the world a safer and healthier place.

REFERENCES

American Council on Education (ACE), Art & Science Group LLC, and the College Board . (2008). *College-bound students' interest in study abroad and other international learning activities.* Baltimore, MD: Art & Science Group.

Boulden, K. (2022). Black student experiences with study abroad marketing and recruitment. *Frontiers: The Interdisciplinary Journal of Study Abroad, 34*(2), 205-234.

Carlson, J. S., & Widaman, K. F. (1988). The effects of study abroad during college on attitudes toward other cultures. *International Journal of Intercultural Relations, 12*(1), 1-17.

Comp, D. (2016). A historical overview of international education scholarship and the role ofthe scholar-practitioner. In B. Streitwieser & A. C. Ogden (Eds.), *International highereducation's scholar-practitioners: Bridging research and practice*, 73-91. Oxford, UK: Symposium Books.

Comp, D. (2020). History of undergraduate research abroad. In K. M. Patch & L. M. Berends(Eds.), *Undergraduate research abroad: Approaches, models, and challenges*, 18-22.Washington, D.C.: NAFSA: Association of International Educators.

Durbin, R. J. (2006). The Lincoln Commission and the future of study abroad. *International Educator, 15*(1), 4.

Dwyer, M. M. (2004). More is better: The impact of study abroad program duration. *Frontiers: The interdisciplinary journal of study abroad, 10*, 151-163.

European Commission (2017, January 26). *Memo: From Erasmus to Erasmus +: A story of 30 years.*
https://ec.europa.eu/commission/presscorner/detail/en/MEMO_17_83

Faupel, C. (2021). *A historical analysis of US-based study abroad program providers.* [Unpublished doctoral dissertation]. University of South Carolina.

FISU. (2023). *About FISU: The international university sports federation (Fédération internationale du sport universitaire).* https://www.fisu.net/fisu/about-fisu/

FISU. (2021). *FISU healthy campus best practices 2021.* https://www.fisu.net/medias/fichiers/healthy_campus_interactive_e_book.pdf

Forum on Education Abroad. (2021). *Guidelines: Advancing the United Nations sustainable development goals through education abroad.* https://www.forumea.org/advancing-the-un-sustainable-development-goals-through-education-abroad.html

Fulbright, J. W. (1976). Convocation address: The process of humanizing mankind. In R.J. Armbruster (Ed.), *A process of global enlightenment, International education: Link for human understanding. A report of the Bicentennial project marking the thirtieth anniversary of the educational exchange program under the Fulbright-Hays Act.* Board of Foreign Scholarships.

Hoffa, W. (2007). *A history of US study abroad: Beginnings to 1965.* Forum on Education Abroad.

Hoffa, W. & DePaul, S. (2010). *A history of US study abroad: 1965 to the present.* Forum on Education Abroad.

Hubbard, A., & Rexeisen, R. J. (2020). Investing in study abroad and cultural engagement: A win-win for career development. *Frontiers: The Interdisciplinary Journal of Study Abroad, 32*(3), 3-21.

Institute of International Education. (2022). *U.S. study abroad.* https://opendoorsdata.org/data/us-study-abroad/

NAFSA. (2002). *Interorganizational task force on safety and responsibility in study abroad: Responsible study abroad: Good practices for health and safety.* https://www.nafsa.org/sites/default/files/media/document/responsible-study-abroad.pdf

NAFSA. (1998). *Responsible study abroad: Health and safety guidelines: Statement of purpose.* https://www.nafsa.org/sites/default/files/media/document/responsible-study-abroad-1998.pdf

International Olympic Committee. (2023). *What are the Olympic values?* https://olympics.com/ioc/faq/olympism-and-the-olympic-movement/what-are-the-olympic-values

Kuh, G. (2008). *High-impact educational practices: What they are, who has access to them, and why they matter.* American Association of Colleges and Universities (AAC&U).

Lopez-McGee, L., Comp, D., & Contreras, E. (2018). Diversity in education abroad: A review of contemporary research and future opportunities. In H. Barclay Hamir & N. Gozik (Eds.) *Inclusive excellence in education abroad: A handbook of theory and practice*, 17-41. Sterling, VA: Stylus Publishing, LLC.

Mandela, N. (2003, July 16). *Speech commemorating the launch of Mindset Network, a group working to improve education and health in South Africa.* http://www.mandela.gov.za/mandela_speeches/2003/030716_mindset.htm

National Center for Education Statistics (NCES). (2022). *Total undergraduate fall enrollment in degree-granting postsecondary institutions, by attendance status, sex of student, and control and level of institution: Selected years, 1970 through 2031.* https://nces.ed.gov/programs/digest/d22/tables/dt22_303.70.asp

Netz, N., Klasik, D., Entrich, S. R., & Barker, M. (2020). Socio-demographics: A global overview of inequalities in education abroad participation. *Education abroad*, 28-42.

Olympic Museum (2023). Olympism and the Olympic movement: What is Olympism?
https://stillmed.olympic.org/media/Document%20Library/OlympicOrg/Documents/Document-Set-Teachers-The-Main-Olympic-Topics/Olympism-and-the-Olympic-Movement.pdf/

Paige, R. M., Fry, G. W., Stallman, E. M., Josić, J., & Jon, J. E. (2009). Study abroad for global engagement: The long-term impact of mobility experiences. *Intercultural Education*, *20*(Suppl.1), S29-S44.

Pulse International. (2022, January). *White Paper: International safety and security positions in higher ed.* https://www.pulseinternational.org/resources

Raby, R. L., & Rhodes, G. M. (2018). Promoting education abroad among community college students: Overcoming obstacles and developing inclusive practices. In *Promoting Inclusion in Education Abroad* (pp. 114-132). Routledge.

Rhodes, G. M. (1995). The Internet and World Wide Web: Uses for study abroad. *Frontiers: The Interdisciplinary Journal of Study Abroad*, *1*, 108-12.

Rhodes, G., Loberg, L., & Hubbard, A. (2013, November). *The many responsibilities of a study abroad administrator. Terra Dotta newsletter*, Chapel Hill, North Carolina.

Streitwieser, B., & Light, G. (2016). The grand promise of global citizenship through study abroad: The student view. In *Global and local internationalization* (pp. 67-73). Brill.

SUNY COIL Center. (2023). *What is COIL?* https://system.suny.edu/global/coil-center/

Sutton, R. C., & Rubin, D. L. (2004). The GLOSSARI project: Initial findings from a system-wide research initiative on study abroad learning outcomes. *Frontiers: The Interdisciplinary Journal of Study Abroad, 10*(Fall), 65-82.

Senate Resolution 308 (109th) (2005, November 10): A resolution designating 2006 as the "Year of Study Abroad." Washington, D.C.

Stroud, A. H. (2010). Who plans (not) to study abroad? An examination of US student intent. *Journal of Studies in International Education, 14*(5), 491-507.

Valuy, E., & Shao, Y. (2021, October). *A legacy of supporting excellence and opportunity in study abroad: 20 year impact study.* Institute of International Education.

Author Bios

Gary Rhodes, Ph.D., is a Professor and the Chair of the Graduate Education Division, Coordinator of the Higher Education Administration and Leadership (HEAL) Graduate Certificate Program & Director of the Center for Global Education in the College of Education at California State University at Dominguez Hills (CSUDH). Prior to that, he was Associate Dean, International at CSUDH (2015 – 2018); Director of the Center for Global Education at UCLA (2010 – 2015), Director of the Center for Global Education and Designed International Student Outreach at Loyola Marymount University (2004 – 2010), Interim Director of the University of California Education Abroad Program Office at UCLA (2003 - 2004), Director of the Center for Global Education at the University of Southern California (USC) (1998 – 2004); Program Coordinator in the Office of Overseas Studies (1989 – 1998) at USC; and Graduate Assistant and Interim Technical Advisor for the Support to Primary Education Project in Cameroon for USC (1988 – 1989). He is on the Executive Board of the US and International Pierre de Coubertin

Committees (Coubertin is the founder of the Modern Olympics). As Director, Center for Global Education (www.globaled.us: 1998 – Present) he has been awarded many grants, done research, developed resources, & published and presented widely on education abroad issues; including health & safety, legal issues, integrated learning before, during & after study abroad, as well as international learning & understanding through the Olympic movement & the United Nations Sustainable Development Goals. He received Fulbright Specialist Awards to India and South Africa. He earned his graduate degrees at USC and his undergraduate degree at the University of California at Santa Barbara. Email: garymrhodes@gmail.com

Lisa Loberg, Ed.D., is the Associate Director of Exchange and Study Away at Art Center College of Design in Southern California. She has nearly 20 years of experience in international education, leading offices and developing institutional partnerships and programs abroad. Her experience also includes a Semester at Sea in 2014 as Outreach Coordinator for the fall voyage. Lisa serves as the private institution representative for California Study Abroad (Cal Abroad), a regional organization for study abroad professionals throughout California. She was a co-founder of the Lessons From Abroad organization (LFA), which continues to provide networking opportunities, re-entry programming, and resources, along with regional conferences to support study abroad returnees throughout the United States. She is also a Research Associate for The Center for Global Education, an international resource center for faculty, staff, students, and families. She currently serves on the advisory boards for the American Institute for Foreign Study (AIFS) and the American College of the Mediterranean (ACM). She earned her Master's in French from Boston College, where she also got her start teaching and working in study abroad, and Ed.D. in Educational Leadership from the University of California, Los Angeles. Her research examines factors of student participation in study abroad. Email: lisaloberg1@gmail.com

Chapter 2

International Education

How Did We Get Here?

Michael B. Smithee, Ed.D.
Syracuse University (retired), Smithee Associates, LLC, United States

ABSTRACT

What follows are my recollections of how international education evolved in the nearly 50 years of my engagement in the field. This personal view of what happened in the development of the field comes from my experiences before and after starting my career. I will also include my recollections of how the term "international educators" arose, technological changes, events, and circumstances along the way that influenced our thinking about the field and its members: international educators. Spoiler Alert: We got here because people and organizations in the field before and after the year 2000 had a vision and displayed both an urgency and patience that required pivoting and resilience to deliver the knowledge and processes to make the field stable and viable.

Keywords: Concepts, Definitions, Events, International Education Evolution, Leadership, Profession

Mobility and Exchanges

Let's start with mobility and exchanges. Before WWII, the United States was not considered the world power it is today, one that serves as a protector of free nations. After WWII, the mobility of higher education students worldwide began to change significantly. Studying abroad, considered more of a perk for the rich, began to mobilize as an exchange of students and faculty for education and research. Although study abroad continued to be thought of as a junior or post-graduation year abroad that mostly women engaged in as part of their maturation process, changes came in supporting educational exchange.

Through the Fulbright Act of 1946, mobility among higher education students and faculty worldwide was envisioned to emphasize how democracies functioned. This vision has since expanded and evolved to shape foreign policy through international exchanges. More recently, the evolution of international education shifted from the management of individual exchanges to an emphasis by higher education institutions on global learning and global competencies. This engendered physical as well as virtual engagement with national and cultural differences.

The Ideal of International Education - The Great Society and IEA-66

In 1970, toward the end of my graduate studies in International Relations at Florida State University (FSU), I attended a government career fair in which I received a copy of the Selected Readings to Supplement of the International Education Act of 1966 (Brademas, 1966). This detailed set of readings supported President Lyndon Johnson's Great Society Program and its vision of international education. It became a foundational resource for me in my quest to work in the field of international education.

Three bills comprised the Great Society vision. These were the Civil Rights, Voting Rights, and International Education Acts. President Lyndon Johnson provided the rationale for International Education. In his message to Congress, he explained that the U.S. government sought to strengthen international education cooperation, stimulate educational exchange with other nations, assist in aiding development in other nations, and build new bridges of international understanding. Although many academics and community members at large wrote in support of this legislation, the International Education Act of 1966 was the only one of the three Bills that was never funded. The Vietnam War intruded. Without funding, it was left to various academic institutions and individual government departments to create the linkages and curricula. So, there we were, rather than being unified, we were adrift. (Smithee, 2012).

Fragmentation of IEA-66 or a Backdoor to International Education

As I was majoring in International Relations at FSU, I was so pleased to see anything international recognized as an essential element in our lives. The many writers included in the IEA-66 Readings became my initial guideposts. The vision of international education only attained broad higher education buy-in through various stakeholders, governmental and non-governmental grants, and funds that benefited Universities as a whole. These grants tended to focus on area studies (Middle East, Southeast Asia, for example) or exchanges of faculty and then students. These backdoor sources of funding dried up by August 1970. Consequently, I could not find a job anywhere in the field, resulting in a five-year gap in my international education journey. However, in January 1976, at 32 (far later than most of my peers), I began my career as an international educator in the International Student Office at Syracuse University.

One result of not funding the IEA-66 Act was that the higher education institutional approach to international education remained tied to academic departments and their research and curriculum. International offices, in contrast, would have to rely on legal, programming, and study abroad approaches to demonstrate their worth in the institution. Often, programming was an adjunct to and usually justification for the critical nature of the legal setting.

Developing Educational Programs

At that time, I did not consider myself an *international educator*. Educator, yes, since I had spent the previous five years teaching middle and high school students. However, I spent the first ten years of my SU career incorporating my experience in teaching, developing, and administering programs involving international students and international concepts in the university and community. My background as a teacher was invaluable in this aspect of international education. Still, the term international educator was not the title applied to my job. My job and others in the field had titles like Program Coordinator, Foreign Student Advisor, Admissions Specialist, Study Abroad Advisor, and ESL Teacher. However, I did bring my background of growing up in many and varied U.S. states, being in the U.S. Army, being stationed abroad, having a dual degree in International Relations and Political Science, and five minors in the social sciences. All of these led me to pursue a doctorate in Higher Education.

Since I was on the international student side of the field, rather than the study abroad side, my focus was not so much on domestic mobility abroad but on finding ways to engage foreign students and Americans meaningfully with each other. My challenges were with the types of programs that could make meaningful engagement between Americans and international students. I realized that programs such as International Week, various country holidays, and so on were important to international students. So, I supported and assisted them. But I really liked programs that allowed for meaningful exchanges, such as the dinners with American families, the visits of students to local schools, and the International Living Center. During this time, the name "international student" began to be used more frequently, as the term "foreign student" was often considered embarrassing and disrespectful.

To some degree, these programs fit between what I call the high and low road for international education. Whereas the IEA-66 was the high road to the internationalization of education, the low road focused on using international programs and recruiting international students for the monetary embellishment of the academic institution. The IEA-66 focused primarily on academic programs, area studies (Middle East, Southeast Asia, etc.), and concepts of international engagement in social and educational programs. While these would contribute to the strong background for a degree, they were not immediately translatable to global competencies. A widespread internationalization or globalization would have to wait nearly 40 years to be conceptualized, advocated for, and integrated into curriculum development, programs, and wholesale campus internationalization, and now often framed as global education, global learning, and global competencies.

Focusing on student (study abroad) mobility, which involved a gain in financial benefits, was a 'low' road characterized as "when you live by the dollar, you die by the dollar." Then, such an approach by university administrators was usually considered a 'cash cow' for other institutional priorities. As such, programs framed in this way poorly served the ideals of international education set out in the IEA-66. This showed that the 'high road' from an institutional and educational (the IEA-66) point of view meant that engaging in international education prepared students and faculty to understand and act on knowledge of the world order and the global environment. The caveat was that each student must make the connections independently in the 'real' world.

The Fulbright program was funded (and often politically attacked). International education was idealized as aiding the U.S. foreign policy objectives while helping development in other nations, albeit from a northern hemisphere and developed nation point of view. One program that has endured is the Peace Corps, in which President Kennedy fostered the idea that we had a duty to help others. Since that time, returning Fulbright and Peace Corps volunteers have contributed significantly to establishing international education as a profession.

Providing Tools for International Education Professionals

How did professionals in international and study abroad offices gain insight into their roles as international educators (even before they knew they were international educators)? From 1976 to 2023, organizations and individuals established themselves as respected leaders in international exchange and international education. Among them, NAFSA: Association of International Educators (NAFSA) stands out (Smithee, 2012).

Advocacy and dissemination of information on international education topics before 1990 relied on printed academic journals, newsletters, newspapers, and conferences. However, we had to wait for the U.S. and campus postal services to deliver these resources. This was our everyday life. Since 1990, technology has broadened our ability to receive and send information with speed and variety of content. In a post-2000 world, a more robust exchange of ideas and advocacy began through various print and, more often, in online publications. Examples are NAFSA's *International Educator*, the *Journal of Studies in International Education*, the *University World News*, and others (Smithee, M. 2022). In addition to providing unity to the field, it became easier to target our audience(s) and generate faster responses to issues and crises as needed, as well as share emerging ideas in the field of international education and even begin to think of ourselves as international *educators.*

These publications contributed immensely to their readers' knowledge base, expanded our knowledge base, and unified our understanding of the vision and what was needed for success. These resources reinforced and supported our sense that engagement between Americans and international students required more than just a brief rubbing of shoulders (the contact hypothesis). In addition, it was thought that study abroad students, by the experience of having lived and studied abroad, would return with a wealth of knowledge about that country and cultural differences. However, study abroad offices struggled to provide seasoned staff time to debrief student returnees. The opportunities I had to collaborate with the study abroad office in conducting such debriefings were well received by the students and study abroad staff. Unfortunately, very few advisors were adept at or had time to implement it.

Establishing the Value of International Education

Articulating the value of international education was and continues to be a complex endeavor. There are many stakeholders: Higher education institutions (HEIs), non-governmental organizations (NGOs), government (Congressional and Executive in particular), faculty, students, parents, international program administrators, and many of the same from other nations. In higher education institutions, the academic departmental view is guided by research, teaching, and recruitment. The non-academic departmental view of the international office is driven by administrative load, ability to provide services, legal issues, and its ability to enhance institutional prestige and advocate for internationalization ideals.

These two forces, as disparate as they seem, found themselves seeking the same goal: the preservation of the international elements of the university or, as some would put it, preserving their jobs. In the early 1990s, higher education institutions, when confronted with the impending reduction of college-bound high school graduates, responded by engaging in a process of *retrenchment.* International offices in many U.S. universities and academic programs were threatened with staff reductions. University administrators were not so aware of the fact that while the trend for the domestic student pipeline was declining, the trend for international students was rising. Thus, our office was slated to lose one advisor and 1.5 staff. This would create a severe problem in our serving rising numbers of international students.

It was here that hard data was needed to justify the value of international education. Rather than provide academic arguments based on education and social benefits, data was needed that showed the importance of international student increases, educationally through graduate teaching and research assistants and monetarily through sheer numbers. The resolution to the conundrum for our office came from a unique source. My graduate assistant also happened to be president of the Graduate Student Organization at the University. In her position, she had weekly meetings with the Chancellor (something I could not do). She presented to the Chancellor some data that I provided. This data was in the form of the net income generated by international graduate and undergraduate students and their families, less the assistantships and other remuneration and grants given by the university to them. The conclusion showed that the net benefit of international students and their families was 20 million dollars. She then asked the Chancellor which academic departments would be diminished if the current and future international students and their parents were told before arrival that the international office could not provide them services. The Chancellor recognized the problem and reversed the staff reduction. Later, after further data gathering, our staff was increased.

If retrenchment was an alert, the Asian financial crisis in the late 90s was a strong wake-up call. I think the retrenchment experience led to our university's positive management of the Asian crisis, as did many other universities. This crisis further established international education as an essential element of the universities, if only due to the bottom line.

I also believe these crises showed that international education was ready for a seat at the table. How this seat was managed varied by institution. A common thread for many institutions was creating an upper-level administrative place for a Senior International Officer. However, the broader picture is that universities use international students to solve domestic problems. Now, it was time for those institutions to fully vest an international dimension in their institutional mission. While this avenue is still under construction, the American Council on Education has invested in an Internationalization Laboratory. This has incorporated a deep dive into institutional capacities for internationalization. (ACE, 2023).

Understanding Ourselves as a Profession

NAFSA: Association of International Educators

The 1980s saw significant changes in NAFSA leadership and professionalization. However, advocacy continued to be an essential element of NAFSA's mission. Until the mid-1980s, there was a conflict between the rules governing the monies NAFSA received from the government and the outreach and advocacy conducted by NAFSA to improve immigration regulations, visa issuance, and other hot issues. Also, by the mid-1980s, NAFSA used governmental funds to professionalize itself and its members. While professionalization was instrumental to the growth of international education, the downside to these governmental linkages was a rule that by receiving governmental funds, grants, etc., one could not advocate or lobby the government for change. At the time, advocacy was NAFSA's bread and butter. However, this rule still applies today (U.S. HHS, 2023).

At the same time, it became clear that NAFSA's full name, National Association of Foreign Student Affairs, was inappropriate for the membership it served or the image it wanted to portray. In 1989, after much discussion by the NAFSA Board of Directors, of which I was a member, it was voted to change the name to NAFSA: Association of International Educators. I wrestled with this meaning because I thought it overshot what we did, but I also thought it served as a goal for members to expand their conceptualization of what they do. At that time, I didn't think most members would consider themselves educators. In hindsight, I see the wisdom of this name change. It is the only international organization with the word 'educator' in its title. As of 2023, I have found that many people now use the term *International Educator* to identify their work. (Smithee, 2015).

Continuing to Wrestle with Definitions

Defining internationalization. Part of the quest to anchor international education on campuses focused on definitions. Is it an academic term? Is it a goal? Is it a policy objective? Is this what an international educator does? Not so fast. One often spoke not of international education but of how the campus was "internationalized." Our campus and collective national efforts sought to broaden and amend the university's mission to include recognition of the international dimensions of the campus. Unification of these dimensions was, for many universities, a real challenge. While the organizational change issues played out, other efforts were emerging. These efforts were often tied to learning to communicate with others or *intercultural communication*. Many authors published books and had leadership positions in organizations connected to aspects of international education. They played their role in advancing organizational and intercultural ideals to higher education structures. In the 1980s, we named the organizational and intercultural efforts *Internationalizing the University.*

Still, what was lacking was a cogent definition. For too long the term, *internationalization* languished in a traditional state. It was thought of as a goal or a result, an area of study much as the concepts of the IEA-66 Readings seemed to suggest. However, a Canadian, Dr. Jane Knight, in 2003, first articulated that internationalization is a ***process***, not a goal, not a set of concepts. (Knight, J. 2003). From then on, researchers, observers, and writers began to utilize this idea to formulate training and develop advocacy for change. Between 1990-2010, other academics, researchers, and practitioners paved the way for a more complex broadening and understanding of the complex nature of international education. In 2011, Dr. John Hudzik (who represented all three) expanded this articulation of internationalization by establishing a new framework. NAFSA published this as *Comprehensive Internationalization: From Concept to Action* (Hudzik, 2011). He wrote of guiding institutions into becoming more globally attuned. By this time, more stakeholders supported the idea. Hudzik and others provided us with the understanding that international education and internationalization were not stand-alone projects. It was a high-level campus-wide conceptualization and process. Hudzik showed how internationalization could and should be part of all aspects of higher education institutions, beginning with a mission statement that reflected a commitment to international education.

Defining and Becoming an International Educator. Another change I have noticed is the increase in academic credentials in the field, especially in the leadership of the field. There are vastly more doctorates in the field in 2023 than in 1980. This gives further legitimacy to using the term international educator, as many practitioners in the field conduct research and hold teaching positions at their institutions. The actual work conducted by international and study abroad offices can be classified as educationally focused. Along with this trend, the NAFSA Board of Directors transformed itself from a primarily practitioner-based body to one that intentionally includes members with skills and experiences, academic and practitioner, that would enable it to lead international education.

Diversity and Multiculturalism. Another aspect of internationalization involved working with issues like diversity and multiculturalism. In my view, NAFSA wrestled with the ideas of internationalization, diversity, and multiculturalism in the 1980s and into the 1990s. In 1990, as my university grappled with retrenchment, the vice president for Student Affairs proposed merging the diversity, multicultural, and international offices into one unit in one space. Our office was charged with developing a response to this idea. Having been on the NAFSA Board of Directors, I knew that NAFSA was wrestling with the same issues. The problem was that NAFSA had difficulty approaching these issues because they couldn't define the differences. I began calling various universities to inquire how these three were organizationally placed. The result was an article for the NAFSA Newsletter in April/May 1991. It was titled *Internationalism, Diversity, and Multiculturalism: Are They Compatible?* (Smithee, 1991). This article helped articulate significant similarities and differences between these concepts and their legal and social differences. We did not merge. Today, while the legal basis for the differences remain, the social, political, and educational differences likely have changed. In another aspect of this topic, I have had the honor of working with a Historically Black College and University (HBCU) (Osakwe, 2017). My research tells me that HBCUs are hearing the call for internationalization. Their focus has been through study abroad but more recently on faculty and internationalization of the curriculum. This publication was titled *Internationalizing the Curriculum for All Learners* (Osakwe, 2022).

The Future

Since I started in 1976, international education has become increasingly relevant in higher education in the U.S. and many other nations. The number of international students coming to the U.S. has doubled but is slightly less since the pandemic. When I started, there were 154,000. In 2018, there were over 1,000,000 (Open Doors, 2023). Visibility became very clear. Ironically, the pandemic opened up the world of virtual education, student advising, and engagement among professionals. Since my 2005 retirement from Syracuse University, research by academics and practitioners on international education has dramatically increased, leading to a vast expansion in published articles on international education. I am very pleased to continue this effort 18 years after my retirement (Smithee, 2022).

My interest and advocacy for international education did not decrease in my retirement. So, enter NAFSA Phase II: Continuing Educators. International educators of my generation and subsequent generations nearing retirement can now maintain contact with colleagues and friends in the field, advocate for the programs they love, and use their knowledge as a consultant. Some Phase II members undertake travel trips together. At the same time, many in Phase II want to continue their contributions to international education by supporting NAFSA and other organizations they care for.

At the 75th annual conference of NAFSA held in May 2023, I heard, in conversations and sessions, many comments such as, "I am an international educator." I heard and read terms like global learning, global citizenship, and globalization. The effort moves beyond the perceived country-to-country (international) engagement to a broader view of engagement. Many institutions like the concept and prestige of having an office of global programs.

If you have made it this far, you know much has been left out. These are my recollections on how international education has evolved. As I continue my involvement in research, learning, and engagement with international education and educators, what can we say about the future of international education?

One element that strikes me is the notion of Internationalization at Home (IaH). This concept takes its impetus from the internationalization of the curriculum. IaH rightly asks, "How do those who do not travel abroad obtain global competencies?" The avenue that IaH proposes is for faculty to modify their courses to include the international perspective. This will engage *all* students in the international dimension of their lives (Smithee, 2022).

Another element of the future will be the increased need for facilitated debriefings of all varieties of international and intercultural engagement, especially as virtual engagement expands. Facilitators experienced in intercultural communication (IC) and DEI will be needed.

I wonder if current and future generations will have the same commitment to international education that I perceive in my generation. We did not see international education as a job; rather, we saw it as a career, mission, profession, or a deep commitment to the ideals of all that is international.

I envision a time when the term *international educator* is more widely understood and defined. To this end, I hope that the term *international educator* will be accepted and have meaning for everyone.

REFERENCES

American Council on Education. (2023). *ACE Internationalization Laboratory*. https://www.acenet.edu/Programs-Services/Pages/Professional-Learning/ACE-Internationalization-Laboratory.aspx

Brademas, J., Perkins, C., Green, E., Thompson, F., Holland, E., Dent, J., Pucinski, R., Daniels, D., O'Hara, J., Powell, A., Scott, R., Carey, H., Hawkins, A., Sickles, C., Gibbons, S., Ford, W., Hathaway, W., Mink, P., Scheuer, J., Meeds, L.,...& Erlenborn, J. (1966). *International education: Past, present, problems and prospects. Selected Readings to Supplement H. R. 14643. House Document Number527*, pp. 528–545. https://eric.ed.gov/?id=ED087643

Hudzik, J. (2011). *Comprehensive internationalization: From concept to action*. https://www.nafsa.org/bookstore/comprehensive-internationalization-concept-action.

Knight, J. (2003). Updated definition of internationalization. *International Higher Education*, (33). https://doi.org/10.6017/ihe.2003.33.7391

NAFSA. (2023). *Phase II: Continuing educators MIG*. https://network.nafsa.org/communities/community-home?CommunityKey=1fbb46ab-fee4-4c2d-b01c-928788a9dacb

Open Doors. (2023). *Enrollment trends*. https://opendoorsdata.org/data/international-students/enrollment-trends

Osakwe, N. (Ed.). (2022). Internationalizing the curriculum for all learners. *Journal of Phi Beta Delta Honor Society for International Scholars, 11*(2), Spring/Summer 2022. irr.2022.final.ready.for.web.pdf (phibetadelta.org)

Osakwe, N. (Ed.). (2017). Internationalizing the curriculum. *Journal of Phi Beta Delta Honor Society for International Scholars, 6*(2). https://bit.ly/3ar8CK1

Smithee, M. B. (2022). Advancing internationalization through faculty publication of their experiences in internationalizing the curriculum at historically black colleges and universities. In K. Bista & A. Pinder (Eds.), *Reimagining internationalization and international initiatives at historically black colleges and universities*. Springer. PP. 141-158. https://link.springer.com/chapter/10.1007/978-3-030-96490-0_9

Smithee, M. B. (2015). *What is an international educator? Smithee Associates: A focus on international education.* WordPress. https://wordpress.com/view/smitheeassociates.wordpress.com

Smithee, M. B. (2012). Finding leadership for the internationalization of U.S. higher education.

Journal of International Education and Leadership, 2(1). http://www.jielusa.org/home

Smithee, M. B. (1991). Internationalism, diversity, and multiculturalism: Are they compatible? *NAFSA: Association of International Educators*, 2(46). https://www.academia.edu/1215423/

U.S. Health and Human Services. (2023). Federal restrictions on lobbying for HHS financial assistance recipients.
https://www.hhs.gov/grants-contracts/grants/grants-policies-regulations/lobbying-restrictions.html

Author Bio

Michael B. Smithee, Ed.D., is an international educator, intercultural trainer, and journal editor. For 30 years, he served as an international educator and taught at Syracuse University. Also, during this time, he served in a variety of elective positions in NAFSA, resulting in his being awarded Life Membership in NAFSA. Since retiring from the university in 2005, he has consulted on internationalization with institutions abroad and nationally, including HBCUs. His publications include topics on the meaning of being an international educator, internationalizing the curriculum, leadership in international education, intercultural academic integrity, U.S. classroom culture, and cross-cultural crisis management. He received his doctorate in higher education from Syracuse University. In addition, he is the editor-in-chief of the *Journal International Research and Review, Journal of Phi Beta Delta Honor Society for International Scholars*. Email: ms@smitheeassociates.com

Chapter 3

Realizing Internationalization's Fullest Potential for Transforming the 21st Century Academy

Reflections of an Old-Timer

Harvey Charles, Ph.D.
University of Minnesota, USA

ABSTRACT

Colleges and universities have a unique role to play in responding to the global challenges and opportunities of the 21st century, and international education is ideally suited to lead in this regard. Yet, be it in terms of financing, the selection of appropriate leadership, a preoccupation with student mobility, an insufficient engagement with DEI, or the absence of a full embrace of global learning, international education continues to fail to realize its fullest potential in the academy. That the field has developed its own body of professional practice and knowledge means that SIOs have a map to guide their work, which can ultimately lead to the institutionalization of international education on campuses. In this regard, the SIO has an increasingly indispensable role to play—a role that can only help to assure greater relevance and success for those institutions that embrace a robust and strategic internationalization agenda.

Keywords: Global Competence, Global Engagement, Higher Education, International Education, Justice, Equity, Diversity, and Inclusion (JEDI), Senior International Officer

Introduction

Among the 24 key characteristics of world-class universities as listed by *The Challenge of Establishing World-Class Universities* (Salmi, 2009), at least 15 of them make explicit reference to international matters. In effect, institutions at the cutting edge of research and teaching are those that must, of necessity, be globally engaged and similarly committed to preparing globally competent graduates. This vision has been the central animating factor in my career as an international educator because I have repeatedly seen how this institutional posture has led to transformation in the lives of students, faculty, and even campuses. Indeed, I have been transformed by this work myself, gaining a much deeper understanding of how our interconnected and interdependent world impacts human experience, and as a consequence, how higher education must respond to this new and evolving reality. The institutionalization of international education represents one of the imperatives that higher education must navigate to achieve an alignment between the needs of societies and the work of the academy. How we prepare students, the kinds of questions that scholarship seeks to answer, and the ways in which we serve the communities we inhabit must resonate with the immediate and evolving realities that we face and can anticipate. This essay will reflect on the perspectives I have gained during the course of my career and the issues that I believe must be attended to in order to ensure that international education occupies a more central place in the ecosystem of colleges and universities as we move deeper into the 21st century.

Student Mobility's Enduring Role in International Education

International education in the early 1990s was still trying to define itself. The conversations that dominated the discourse in this field involved study abroad as the pathway to develop intercultural competence, and international students as a way to promote cultural diversity on college campuses. Thirty years later, study abroad and the presence of international students are still the reflexive reaction to the subject of international education, but the concerns they precipitate are different. With study abroad, to the extent that it is embraced, the preference is now for shorter experiences abroad, often led by faculty—a significant shift from the semester- and year-abroad experiences that tended to be the norm a few decades ago. There have also been greater efforts to both expand education abroad to include internships and research abroad, and to tie the education abroad experience more closely to the curriculum. With respect to the presence of international students, the overwhelming concern across much of the academy has to do with how more of them can be recruited, given the important role that the tuition revenues they provide have become to the budgets of both public and private institutions. For all intents and purposes, there is now an all-out scramble for international student tuition dollars, one that is happening as international student enrollment in the U.S. is declining. A veritable industry of private agents and organizations has sprung up to assist institutions in recruiting international students and institutions desperate to attract as many of these students as possible. This phenomenon is one conspicuous example of the encroachment of commercialization within the academy in general and in the context of internationalization in particular—a trend that, while having some merits, is disturbing in many other ways. Beyond these concerns, however, there are doubts as to whether the practice of depending on tuition revenues from international student enrollment is sustainable for all post-secondary institutions. Contrary to popular thinking among university leadership, it is not a quick fix to fill budgetary gaps, and this will prove to be particularly true for less highly ranked institutions in the coming years.

Sustainability as a Core Element of Internationalization

The world of the 21st century faces crises that are practically all global in scope and require global collaboration to find solutions. The sustainable development goals articulated by the United Nations speak to these global challenges in very compelling ways, yet many colleges and universities lack an explicit commitment to prepare students to be globally competent. Some institutions have adopted initiatives that encourage students to engage with grand global challenges, others have programs like Model United Nations, while others embed an internationally focused living and learning community in residence halls. What is absent on many campuses, however, is a conspicuous, explicit, and strategic commitment to global learning. The senior international officer (SIO) is the one administrator who has a campus-wide mandate to champion this agenda. The degree to which such an agenda is accommodated varies from campus to campus. This continues to be an area where important advocacy work has to be done, particularly in terms of internationalizing the curriculum.

International Education Leadership in the Academy

Thankfully, international education as a field is now much more mature even if not quite yet institutionalized at colleges and universities in the U.S. More institutions are now willing to hire a senior administrator to provide oversight of and exploit to the extent possible, the opportunities created by globalization. Although there is a great degree of variation in how this role is understood and articulated on campuses, the acceptance of the need for an administrator to lead internationalization is an important development within the field. There continues to be the issue, however, of who is hired to provide international education leadership. It is still quite common to see SIOs hired who do not have a background in the field of international education. Faculty in areas such as modern languages, international affairs, or faculty who are foreign born are often identified as the ones most suitable for this position. There is often a clear preference for faculty in this role, and while this is not a problem in and of itself, it is very difficult for faculty members to acquire the expertise in international education leadership while teaching and engaging in research activity. Unknown to many who are in the position of hiring international education leaders on campuses, the field of international education has its own body of professional practice and knowledge, and individuals who are hired into this role without a grounding in this area of experience deny their institutions the chance to realize their fullest potential in this area of leadership. Indeed, over the past 15 years, several programs offering graduate degrees in international education have become available. Opportunities to pursue leadership roles in the field are therefore no longer confined to those who are tenured professors, which for decades was typically the only pathway to becoming an SIO. Professionals now have the opportunity to earn a doctorate in the field and combined with practical experience, seek to compete for such roles. This is a fortuitous development, and campuses that seek to pursue internationalization in a strategic manner will best be served by professionals with deep experience in international education leadership.

International Education and Social Justice

The most forceful social justice movement, occurring in the wake of the police killing of George Floyd, prompted a significant degree of introspection in the field in terms of the extent to which international education engages or, at a minimum, is concerned with issues of justice, equity, diversity and inclusion (JEDI). That international educators historically have been viewed by administrators in the JEDI space as aloof and elitist is not surprising. Not only have the majority of administrators in the field of international education been overwhelmingly white, but the JEDI agenda has been perceived as a mostly domestic agenda, and therefore quite apart from the cross-cultural understanding agenda championed by SIOs that generally speaks to the international domain. And yet, JEDI is very much a global issue, as the worldwide protests in the wake of George Floyd's killing demonstrated. Furthermore, international education and multicultural education are two sides of the same coin. The gaze of one may be focused beyond borders and that of the other within borders, but in important ways, many of the issues are the same. That international education has moved to a closer embrace of JEDI is an important development in the field. Institutions would be substantially enriched if both areas pursue intentional collaboration as a way to advance global learning and a deeper commitment to the ideals and the practice of JEDI.

Leveraging Computer Technology to Advance Internationalization

The pandemic has allowed the academy to adopt practices overnight that previously were broadly treated with indifference or even contempt. Practiced universally during the pandemic, online education allowed for instruction to continue mostly uninterrupted, except in circumstances where institutions did not have the appropriate infrastructure or students did not have devices to participate. From K-12 through graduate school, from industrialized countries to the developing world, from far-flung rural communities to crowded urban centers, virtual learning continued despite the need for isolation. By the end of the pandemic, instructors had so much facility with the technology, students had become so accustomed to the medium, and administrators were so pleased with the significant financial savings, that online education now seems to have become a permanent part of the instructional portfolio across the academy. This unprecedented and devastating global phenomenon had the unanticipated effect of boosting global learning strategies like Collaborative Online International Learning (COIL). From its inception, COIL has been based on using distance learning technologies to bring classrooms separated by borders together. Will COIL become an indispensable tool in the arsenal of international educators to help advance global learning? Will virtual education abroad become a reasonable alternative for students who would rather not leave home? The jury is still out on these questions, but what is clear is that the menu of options for engaging globally has expanded and international educators now have more opportunities to advocate for curriculum internationalization with practices that also happen to be much more affordable.

Insularity and Nationalism as Threats to the Internationalization Project

As efforts to further institutionalize practices around justice, equity, diversity, and inclusion have increased, so too has the backlash to these ideas. The recent Supreme Court decision banning affirmative action in the admission decisions at institutions of higher education is a very visible and consequential instance of these sentiments, but state governments, school boards, and other entities have been doing their part to marginalize or even eradicate efforts to make our institutions of learning more receptive to JEDI values. As has been established earlier, in many ways international education is adjacent to JEDI. There has already been hostility shown toward nations like China in terms of scholarly collaboration. The issuance of visas for international students to study in the U.S. has fallen over the past six years. The opposition to efforts to address global challenges like climate change continues notwithstanding the overwhelming evidence of lives being disrupted on a global scale. The demonization of international students, particularly Asian students in the wake of the pandemic, is yet another example of a national mood that is undermining an agenda that supports global engagement as a necessary condition for global understanding and ultimately a more peaceful and prosperous world. International educators must be vigilant about these trends, and stimulate conversations, and create conditions on the campuses they inhabit to promote cross-cultural or multicultural understanding.

The Challenge of Financing Internationalization

Possibly the most accurate indicator for the support that international education enjoys in the academy is the degree to which funding is made available. In the recently concluded Association of International Education Administrators (AIEA) survey among Senior International Educators, financing was identified as the number one challenge they face. While this is a challenge faced by most areas within colleges and universities, it is particularly difficult for the field of international education where many SIOs are expected to generate part or all of their financial revenues from fees. Whether it be from international students, study abroad students, intensive English language tuition, or grant activity, the dependence on "soft" money to fund international education activity is ubiquitous in this field. Clearly, this kind of financing is contingent, and the message to leaders of international education is that this dimension of the academy can only be viable if they pay their own way. Making internationalization a strategic priority of the institution is a necessary step to regularize its financing. This in turn allows international education to engage in its transformative work, and in the process become institutionalized. Institutions that ensure adequate funding for internationalization will find not only that this work thrives, but that their institutions are more aligned with delivering a 21st century education.

Conclusion

International education has grown and matured on college campuses over the past 30 years. It now occupies a much larger and more important footprint in the academy. Its importance, if not readily acknowledged, is implicitly understood in how research is currently conducted through global networks, in how institutions are able to exploit global opportunities and mitigate challenges precipitated by global developments. We effectively live in a global age. Institutions that embrace a robust and strategic internationalization agenda will have a bright future. Those that don't will become irrelevant and fall by the wayside. The SIO will therefore have an increasingly indispensable role to play in helping institutions navigate our global reality.

REFERENCE

Salmi, J. (2009). *The challenge of establishing world-class universities.* The World Bank.

Author Bio

Harvey Charles, Ph.D., is the Vice Provost for International Programs and Senior International Officer for the University of Minnesota system. He is an experienced administrator and scholar in the field of international higher education. Email: hcharles@umn.edu

Chapter 4

Discourses, Imposters, and Quantum Theory

Reflections on Education Abroad

Lance M. Kenney
Honors Department, Villanova University, Pennsylvania, United States

ABSTRACT

In reflecting on the history of education abroad (EA) and the field's future, this paper posits two theoretical models. First, in thinking about the past, I utilize French philosopher Michel Foucault's notion of the dispositif to analyze how the profession became an 'epistemic community.' Second, in looking forward, I highlight EA's continued embeddedness with positivist social science research and propose a different model: quantum theory. Instead of being wed to Newtonian metaphors around concepts like 'cause and effect,' quantum physics gives us different ways of looking at the praxis of the student experience associated with EA, providing a different theoretical lens that is more qualitative in its scope.

Keywords: Dispositifs, Foucault, Imposter Syndrome, Quantum Theory

(T)o stand on the meeting of two eternities, the past and future....
Henry David Thoreau

The Girl from Ipanema

Astrud Gilberto passed away on June 5, 2023, outside Philadelphia (her residence in the area was a surprise to many Philadelphians). Best known for her English-language vocals on "The Girl from Ipanema," Gilberto became an overnight sensation in 1964, and went on to record over a dozen albums, ultimately receiving a Latin Grammy Lifetime Achievement Award.

I was of course sad to hear of Ms. Gilberto's passing, but the constant airing of her most famous song in the weeks after her death brought a smile to my face, as it is a song I associate with my time as an international educator. The highlight of any professional conference was always the opportunity to get together with like-minded "theory heads," to discuss the application of various critical theories to education abroad. Sometimes these conversations translated into conference presentations: one program provider's regional director from France talking about post-structuralism and language acquisition; a resident director from Mexico highlighting the interplay between continental philosopher Julia Kristeva and the "consumption" of culture; a dean of international programs at a large state university teaching me the all-important nuances of postcolonialism in program development. Inevitably, another friend and colleague—the most pragmatic and logical of all of us—would say, "When all of you start talking theory, I always start humming 'Girl from Ipanema' in my head."

In reflecting on my time in the profession, I know I would be driving my friend to hum that great song again. I'm back to theory again. Like Christopher Walken demanding "more cowbell" in the famous *Saturday Night Live* sketch, I'm once more calling for more theory. This volume, in asking practitioners to think back on their time in the profession, is perhaps the first to engage in historiography. Not history *per se*—multiple authors have written histories of the field—but what is the story we have told ourselves about the profession? What is the narrative that we have constructed for ourselves?

My initial thought was to try to categorize the significant events that left an impact on me, but even the terminology was insulting. Do I refer to these phenomena as "phases," "fads," "trends," or "stages"? Even "hot-button topics" seemed derogatory (for instance, increased concern with liability issues shouldn't be marginalized!). The term I landed on, and this is where I have my theory hat back on, is *dispositif*.

The word comes from Michel Foucault (my friends would say, "**of course**") and was used by him in multiple works in multiple contexts. Briefly, dispositifs are "(D)iscourses, institutions, architectural forms, regulatory decisions, laws, administrative measures, scientific statements, philosophical, moral and philanthropic propositions" (Foucault, 1980, p. 194 ff.) that contribute to a body of knowledge, a disciplinary structure, or, for our purposes, a profession. They are "heterogeneous elements," both discursive and non-discursive, that lead to the creation of what another author refers to as an "epistemic community" (Haas, "Introduction," p.2). The concept has been translated many ways by many interlocutors: apparatus, grids of intelligibility, deployment, etc. I think this is one of those wonderful situations where the English does not capture the original essence.

Key *discourses* that have been of importance include those around how we designate ourselves: international, global, cross-cultural, off-campus, student mobility. What are our goals for our students? Intercultural competence, global intelligence, global engagement, global citizenship, enlightened nationalism. How do we achieve this? Writing across cultures, curriculum integration, service-learning, internships, sustainability, reciprocity, internationalization at home, home tuition, learning styles. *Institutions* that come to the forefront include the alphabet soup of professional organizations, some of which no longer have any linkage to the original acronym: NAFSA, AIEA, EAIE, CIEE, IES, and the renamed SECUSSA (though still utilized in practice via the listserv). Architecture certainly features as a dispositif: study centers, branch campuses, international residence halls, homestays, etc. What Foucault calls the "juridico-political" discourse (including *regulations* and *laws*) is probably the most extensive list of dispositifs: the ADA, the Clery Act, "Securing America's Future," and, most recently, GEN-23-03 "Dear Colleague," contribute to the episteme, not to mention constantly-changing visa regulations. Finally, *scientific* statements, particularly medical statements, have perhaps the most bearing: the COVID pandemic continues to have repercussions, but of course it was preceded by H1N1, "avian bird flu," SARS, and monkey pox.

Imposter Syndrome

Another place where Foucault's matrix (versus hierarchy) imagery comes to the forefront is in thinking about the place of the Education Abroad (EA) office in the broader higher education landscape. EA offices are required to work with nearly every other administrative and academic unit on campus. The EA office is also required to act AS those offices. Receiving tuition bills from overseas partners? Bursar. Finding strategies for transferring student loans and grants? Financial assistance. Helping students navigate course selection in the overseas context? Student advising. Making sure that those classes count towards graduation? Registrar. The list goes on and on: career center, student services, health center, residence life, public safety, admissions, intercultural affairs, disability services, learning support. The EA office is in many ways a microcosm of the college/university itself.

However, even a cursory survey of EA offices demonstrates another decades-old debate: where to posit the EA office? Senior level administration? Student affairs? Answering directly to the provost/vice president for academic affairs, or further down the hierarchy, like departmental chairs? In some cases, even as a corollary of the registrar's office. Is the primary function academic? Or student support? How does the field writ large straddle that millennium-old Aristotelian divide between theory (student learning and engagement, pedagogy) and practice (health/safety, liability, standards of practice)? This question around *administrative measures* represents another dispositif that shapes the profession.

Very early in my career it was explained to me that the profession of education abroad is essentially a tripod. It is possible to identify three primary "legs": the campus-based EA office that recruits and sends students; the host university/study center that receives the students; and in many cases the program provider that acts as intermediary. I have been fortunate to have worked in all three areas: at an overseas university responsible for incoming US students; later for a consortium-based program provider, responsible (administratively) for a portfolio of international centers; and then at a campus-based EA office. (It was of course easier to live overseas prior to the War on Terror). What I saw in all three locations was that same nebulous positioning that I have attributed to the EA office itself. What is the role of education abroad? What is its place in higher education generally? When it comes to broader questions of student learning and engagement, does it have a (forgive the cliché) 'seat at the table?' Struggling with the dispositifs that frame the conversation, collectively, the profession seems to be suffering from imposter syndrome.

One consistent way that EA has attempted to "rationalize" itself is through research. The number of peer-reviewed articles published by EA practitioners has grown exponentially in the past thirty years. Most appear in profession-specific journals and rarely, if ever, have a broader impact beyond EA the way, say, Crenshaw's notion of intersectionality impacted non-legal professions or Fukuyama's 'end of history' thesis is read by non-political scientists. However, most do follow tried-and-true social science methodologies: longitudinal analysis, case studies, quantitative analysis, systemic reviews, phenomenographic studies, even the odd chi square. These studies attempt to address the questions that have been with the profession from the start: how does foreign language proficiency increase? What is the bearing of program duration? What are the long-term effects of education abroad? How are professional trajectories impacted?

The underlying criticism here goes past what the South Carolinian first mate on a fishing vessel told me in a calming Southern drawl: "when you're doin' all of the talkin', you only teach yourself what you already know." The broader issue may not be with education abroad, but the social sciences silo in which the profession has elected to put itself (again, in response to the dispositifs). Going back to the overarching question of 'what is the narrative we tell ourselves about ourselves?,' why has EA specifically and international education generally wed itself to this methodology? We have embedded ourselves in a tradition that can be traced to Karl Popper, one where to be 'authentic' in the social sciences, we need to model ourselves after the natural sciences. Newtonian physics becomes the standard by which we measure and assess our students and their success. To paraphrase Popper himself, "prediction, not prophecy."

(The discussion about the misuse in EA of the term "authentic" also has been occurring for decades. My personal favorite was the colleague who referred to the hotel in which we were staying as "authentically Spanish" because the toilet had an ashtray embedded in it.)

In our interactions with EA colleagues, in our relationships with other offices or universities, in our advising and guiding of students, we are dealing with *people*. Most of our dealings come down to phenomena we cannot quantify or empirically measure. An interesting parallel can be drawn with the academic discipline of International Relations (IR). If we think of the key variables that drive discussions of world politics—for instance, nationalism or religion—these are the things that appear least in the literature, precisely because they *can't* be measured.

This leads me to ruminate on the future of the profession, and the continued importance of more normative reflections in terms of education abroad. I believe it may be time for Quantum EA.

Quantum Theory and Education Abroad

Critical theorists have been trying to get away from natural science models for the human and social sciences for decades. Recently, particularly in IR, scholars have abjured what one author calls "natural science envy" altogether. The response, to put it in a crass parlance, has been, "You want science? We got your science." In short, these thinkers have turned away from Newtonian metaphors and physics models to constructs, analogies, and theories found within quantum physics.

I in no way claim to have a firm grasp of quantum physics, and this volume is not the place to attempt either an overview of the field or its impact on modern science. However, three key concepts might be relevant to education abroad.

Entanglement. Entanglement refers to subatomic particles impacting one another regardless of distance—measuring some facet of say, a photon, gives you information about its entangled 'partner' no matter how far away that second photon is (even light years). In short, this concept upends one of the basic premises of classical physics: space doesn't matter.

One of the first professional conferences I attended featured a plenary speaker who advocated for banning students in education abroad programs from using email, so that they could better integrate into the host culture (the snickers in the audience were audible). Thirty years of continued reliance on information technologies have proven that speaker even further misinformed. We may refer to our students as being 'abroad' or 'off-campus,' but do they really leave? Or do they remain entangled, in a situation where utilization of social media platforms means that space really doesn't matter? A quantum approach to EA would dismantle the either/or binary of home/away, perhaps even utilizing those technologies to facilitate learning about the US simultaneously with learning about the host culture.

Wormholes. Also known as Einstein-Rosen Bridges, wormholes theoretically represent another instance of space not mattering, with distant points being connected in spacetime. If one were to think of space as flat, say like a piece of paper, a wormhole would represent folding the piece of paper, pushing a pencil through that paper, and the resulting hole being two places at the same time. Applied to politics, wormholes upend traditional notions of sovereignty being wed to physical space, requiring looking at non-space entities (one author highlights free-trade zones and rebel-held areas as resembling wormholes, given their anomalies regarding questions of power) (Neep, 2017, p. 481).

Arrogantly, years ago I coopted Foucault's notion of "heterotopia" ("other spaces" that exist in spite of or in contrast to their surroundings—think *Cabaret*) to advocate taking a closer look at the spaces our students inhabit. Airports, homestays, study centers all represent these 'other spaces,' and the theoretical model of the wormhole might provide a better construct. As with the notion of entanglement, we could do a better job of looking at students' sojourns, past the "here/there" mindset. Further, challenging sovereignty's "territorial trap," should we rethink how we report where our students are going? Is studying in Galicia the same as studying in Catalonia when we say our students are in "Spain"? Do we conflate Hokkaido and Kansai when we say "Japan?"

The Observer Effect. In quantum physics, the observer effect refers to the disturbance of a system by the mere *act* of observation. Specifically, the famous "double slit" experiment shows that the observation of quantum phenomena by an instrument can change the measured results of the experiment (for an excellent overview, search 'double-slit experiment' at www.space.com). Applying this notion to education abroad, how does the presence of US students in an overseas setting change that environment, not just change the students? What is the impact—the equivalent of the "carbon footprint"—on the system within which the students inhabit?

Thankfully, this is an area where as a profession there have been improvements. Again, a literature review (*Frontiers* and the *Journal of Studies in International Education* spring to mind) archive a number of articles that advocate ethnography, and not traditional social sciences, as models for assessing and interpreting student learning. Even International Relations, a discipline known for being glacial in its response to change, has begun to appreciate the challenges of the "objective observer," and is beginning to move away from the aforementioned "natural science envy" (Brigg & Bleiker, 2010).

Like the field of quantum theory itself, the debate within quantum schools regarding the theory's application as 'analogy' or 'actuality' is too voluminous to posit here. However, quantum is not the future of the social sciences (and higher education, and education abroad), it is the 'now.' "As a fundamental worldview, theory of reality and enabler of new technologies, quantum touches everything, in theory and increasingly in practice." (Der Derian and Wendt, 2020, p. 409). Quantum theory has become truly transdisciplinary, impacting not just physics but biology, chemistry, computer science, and economics. If a historiography of the field allows us to unpack the dispositifs that got us here, it also allows us to think about future contributions from other voices. Education abroad, even international education broadly, needs to begin tackling these substantial quantum ideas, proactively and not reactively.

REFERENCES

Brigg, M., & Bleiker, R. (2010). Autoethnographic international relations: Exploring the self as a source of knowledge. *Review of International Studies, 36*(3), 779-798. doi:10.1017/S0260210510000689

Der Derian, J., & Wendt, A. (2020). Quantizing international relations: The case for quantum approaches to international theory and security practice. *Security Dialogue*: *51*(5), 399-413.

Foucault, M. (1980). The confession of the flesh. In C. Gordon (Ed.), *Power/Knowledge: selected interviews and other writings* (pp. 194-228). Vintage.

Haas, P. (1992). Introduction: epistemic communities and international policy coordination. *International Organization*, *46*(1), 1-35.

Neep, D. (2017). State-space beyond territory: Wormholes, gravitational fields, and entanglement. *Journal of Historical Sociology, 30*(3), 465-495.

Author Bio

Lance M. Kenney entered the field of education abroad in 1995, serving as resident staff for a study abroad consortium in Cheltenham, England. After returning to the United States, he served as a program officer for the consortium before being hired by Villanova University. As Director of International Studies for Villanova (2001-2013), he served in multiple professional capacities, including advisory boards and elected positions. Since 2013, he has served as an adjunct lecturer in the University Honors Program, teaching classes on international relations, political theory, and British culture. His interests, both academically and professionally, center around applications of Critical Theory and continental philosophy to global affairs. Email: lance.kenney@villanova.edu

Chapter 5

Then and Now

Thoughts on Education Abroad

Michael Woolf
Deputy President for Strategic Development, CEACAPA, London, United Kingdom

ABSTRACT

Over the last decades education abroad has become more professional. In contrast, most of the elders came into the field from diverse backgrounds. Professionalization has brought demonstrable benefits but, simultaneously, a greater uniformity of thought. The dominant narrative of the value of education abroad has moved from collective good to individual benefit, from idealism to utilitarianism. Shifts in global politics have also challenged the ideological root of internationalism. Since the 1990s, the emergence of radical nationalisms, and militant parochialism has generated closed ideologies in direct collision with the values of international education. We are, thus, in the business of politics. Despite dark political clouds, we have faith in the inexorable curiosity of the young that will not be restrained by real or metaphorical borders. Mobility of mind and body is an aspiration of thoughtful humanity across the world.

Keywords: Professionalization. Nationalism. Xenophobia. Commodification. Utilitarianism. Ideologies. Idealism.

The Past is a Foreign Country

The past is a foreign country; they do things differently there.
L.P. Hartley, *The Go-Between*

What are those blue remembered hills?
That is the land of lost content,
I see it shining plain,

The happy highways where I went
And cannot come again.
A.E. Housman, *A Shropshire Lad*

Things of course change. Otherwise, there would be no nostalgia, no longing for the "blue remembered hills." The problem is that the past is filtered through a prism of unreliable memories. True or false, true and false, myths emerge that have the power to shape the ways in which we invent reality.

What I think of as the Eden Syndrome is just such a myth, much loved by educators. The past (whenever it was) represented a golden age of scholastic dedication in contrast to the feckless present (whenever it is). Through centuries, educators, from Socrates on, have bemoaned the lazy indifference of their students. I have been tempted by this syndrome, seduced momentarily by delusions of nostalgia. However, in more sober moments, I recall that when I went to university many years ago, I was motivated by urgent imperatives, none of which had any connection with academia. I was not dedicated to the study of the Tudor monarchs or political systems of ancient Mesopotamia, or whatever else I was supposed to be studying.

In contrast, many of our students are demonstrably curious and motivated. They get dressed in the morning, undertake responsible tasks as interns or volunteers, come to classes, engage with unfamiliar environments and ideas. Nevertheless, the Eden Syndrome, despite evidence to the contrary, generates notions of decline. Generation this or that (A, X, Y, Z) do not demonstrate the exemplary commitment of their teachers, nor do they appear to know what their teachers think is important. I suspect that they may know things of which their elders have little awareness.

For all of us the past is another country.

I stumbled into international education in the late 1980s. At that time, most of us were enthusiastic amateurs. We have significantly improved our professional standards. We do less damage than we did in the past. Students arrive with some idea of where they are and benefit from much improved health and safety procedures.

Things are more professional now. It is possible to become qualified in international education through the proliferation of graduate degrees. It may be nostalgic, however, to regret one consequence of this. Most of the elders came into the field (if it was a field then) with degrees in humanities, sciences, social sciences, languages, alchemy, rhetoric, etc. In the interaction between diverse perspectives there was some value: a tendency to combine practice with scholarship, an inclination towards interdisciplinary thought, perhaps something of a richer mix. Professionalization has brought demonstrable benefits and, simultaneously, a greater uniformity of thought.

The most marked alteration, though, is that our narrative has progressively altered in a manner that reflects a shift in global ideologies from collectivism towards individualism. The idea of education abroad as a collective good has gone out of focus: the concept that interactions between young people across borders erode stereotypes, create some sense of a common humanity, an awareness of what unites rather than divides us. William Fulbright's vision of the potential impact of education abroad was inspirational: "the acquisition of empathy - the ability to see the world as others see it, and to allow for the possibility that others may see something we have failed to see, or may see it more accurately" (1989, p.217).

The benefits of education abroad are now described in terms of individual advantages: getting a better job, personal experience, and enhancing résumé. Marketing rhetoric tempts students with the promise of access to a global elite, membership of a state of grace called "global citizenship", and, thus, better jobs and higher starting salaries.

Prioritizing study abroad in this manner requires a conscious act of selective vision which ignores other factors that impact upon earning potential and employability such as student leadership roles, athletics participation, what students study, and, crucially, the perceived status of the institution from which they graduate. It also does not acknowledge the critical impact of class, as outlined by Jason DeParle:

> Despite frequent references to the United States as a classless society, about 62 percent of Americans (male and female) raised in the top fifth of incomes stay in the top two-fifths... Similarly, 65 percent born in the bottom fifth stay in the bottom two-fifths (2012).

The assertion that students start from the same place and move upwards through education abroad is demonstrably flawed. As all good socialists know, privilege is largely inherited. The classless society is an illusion.

Return on investment (ROI) is a recurrent cliché more suited to the language of neo-liberalism. Participants (and their parents) are assured that there are financial benefits in studying abroad, special advantages in "a global job market". Paying for education abroad separates them from their lumpen peers. An experience that was conceived of as a means of bringing young people together is now a mechanism for creating a distinct elite. The idea that education abroad is a critical factor in social mobility has become an article of faith.

Another consequence of this commodification and utilitarianism is the emergence of a false hierarchy of knowledge. According to current orthodoxy, science, technology, engineering, and mathematics (STEM) disciplines are of more economic value than the humanities and social sciences. Political pressures on universities to concentrate their resources in STEM reflect the assumption that graduates in these areas are likely to be more employable and to earn more money. That proposition is not supported by convincing evidence. In the UK, the British Academy's key research findings, in *Qualified for the Future*, include the following:

> Graduates who study AHSS subjects [Arts, Humanities and Social Sciences] are highly employable... AHSS graduates underpin key sectors of the UK economy. Of the ten fastest growing sectors, eight employ more graduates from AHSS than other disciplines...While starting salaries are lower, over the longer term, AHSS graduates make strong progress up the career ladder into roles attracting higher salaries (2020, pp. 5-6).

Furthermore:

There is a common misconception that Science, Technology, Engineering or Maths... students are more likely to get a job ... but closer inspection of multiple data sets ...shows that employment rates differ little by subject (p.8).

It does not take too much intelligence to conclude that if the pro-STEM lobbies were very successful, there could easily be a glut of unemployable mathematicians, chemists, and engineers, which is precisely what has happened in India. Engineering is a popular discipline but, according to Pushkar's analysis of The *India Skills Report* of 2023, less than 60% of graduates in that discipline were "considered employable".

There is, in short, little or no reliable evidence that what students study directly relates to employability. That fact has not diminished the populist political noise that falsely commodifies the value of some forms of knowledge over another.

This assumption undermines a commitment to decolonization of curriculum. Literature is critical to the representation of silenced or muted voices; history, the skills and methodologies required to reveal hidden narratives. In *The Post-Colonial Studies Reader*, of 526 pages only 5 relate to STEM disciplines. The humanities and social sciences are at the heart of postcolonial studies. Rhetoric that privileges STEM disciplines demonstrates neo-colonialist assumptions about the interdependence of technology, science, knowledge, progress, and power.

Much else has changed, of course, over the years for ill and for good. However, the fundamental alteration in the narrative of benefits is unsettling because it appears to have happened almost without being noticed. Education abroad reflects a transition from idealism to utilitarianism. Commodification of the benefits of all education may have been an inevitable consequence of other social alterations but it has impoverished our public discourse, created an environment in which we do not comfortably speak of the values that motivated many of us to commit to the work of education abroad.

Hyperbole and the Politics of Hate

Evolution has made Homo sapiens... a xenophobic creature. Sapiens instinctively divide humanity into two parts, "we" and "they."
Yuval Noah Harari, *Sapiens: A Brief History of Humankind*

The boundary between the darkness and the light was shifting all the time, but too subtly for us to be aware of it, except when it was too late.
Michael Dibdin, *And Then You Die*

The COVID pandemic was an obvious and dramatic threat. That said, education abroad has faced and continues to face a number of challenges that predate and persist beyond that crisis. Convincing colleagues at American universities that programs overseas are of equal academic value to those at home has been a challenge throughout my career. Relatively slow rates of growth in the number of participants suggest that the argument has not been won and that parity of esteem is elusive. Some of this reflects academic prejudice but much is a consequence of self-inflicted wounds.

The rhetoric of education abroad, driven by marketing imperatives, makes inflated claims that undermine credibility. The notion of global citizenship is a prime example of hyperbole. It is also intellectually and educationally unsound. Educational objectives need to be capable of qualification with "less" and "more" reflecting progressive acquisition in the learning process. Thus, students may learn more than they knew before through education abroad. Citizenship, in contrast, is a condition. You cannot be less or more a citizen.

The concept becomes even more problematic when qualified by "global". Global litters the ways in which we promote our endeavors, used to qualify concepts such as competencies, awareness, education. Therein lies a paradox. As an adjective it expresses approval but globalization as a process carries ambiguous associations that evoke unease —threats to community identities, a sense that there are both beneficiaries and victims, reduction of control. In short, global is good. Globalization is worrying.

When 'global' is attached to the notion of citizenship, it suggests a state of grace uniquely conferred by the transformative power of education abroad. Abroad (wherever it is) is invested with quasi-mystic capacities to alter consciousness, unlike the mundane banality of home (wherever that is). Many of the same implications are apparent in the well-intentioned statement that "study abroad changed my life". We tend to welcome this validation but, as we all know, you can change your life anywhere, be it Wolverhampton, or Newark, New Jersey. The passive voice enforces the sense that radical alteration is, as in global citizenship, a consequence of place.

There is a substantial difference in the active voice. In "I changed my life by studying abroad", the emphasis shifts from location to individual who, through active learning, has acquired new insights and enhanced awareness. Demystifying the place aligns with educational principles; students are ultimately responsible for their own learning, wherever that happens.

The focus on inter-cultural or cross-cultural education further distorts teaching and learning. It places a misconception at the heart of education abroad. Simply, countries and cultures do not align. Countries are constructs, created by some combination of accident, war, negotiation, colonial intrusion and so on. European countries invented borders in Africa. The artificiality of national identities is demonstrated across the globe. There is no single version of Belgium, British, or Italian culture; is that to be found in Padova or Palermo? Where is American culture located? Alabama? New York? Countries also come and go. Where is Yugoslavia? What was Yugoslavian culture?

These questions demonstrate the problematic nature of inter and cross-cultural emphases. What we do is take students from America to other countries. Countries and cultures are not the same thing. The only other group who speak of countries as a repository of a national culture are militant nationalists. The illusion of cultural cohesion justifies xenophobia. Foreigners are a threat to the fictitious purity of identity.

There are other unintended consequences. By implication, we tell students that we will help them to negotiate or transcend cultural barriers, to anticipate difficulty, enforced by the idea of leaving the comfort zone of home. We answer a question we have not bothered to ask. To what degree have social and technological resources created similarities rather than differences? To know nothing of worlds elsewhere is to choose parochial isolation. Young people across the world have access to many of the same influences. Media transcend borders: a reality obscured in the illusion that countries are static units of cohesive culture.

Talking about culture also offers a way of avoiding more specific, complex, potentially difficult, conversations about religion, politics, social systems, ideologies, dynamics of change, race, and so on. It offers a safer, anodyne form of discourse. There may be many reasons for this timidity. For one, the concept of safety has expanded beyond the physical to include psychological security. The assumption is that students may be damaged by ideas that challenge their inherited beliefs.

There is also historical context. Modern education abroad emerged at a time when McCarthyism and its aftermath made it safer to talk in nebulous terms about culture rather than grapple with more controversial topics. A mechanism designed to protect teachers from hostile critics evolved into an orthodoxy that has done little to enhance academic credibility.

Right wing hostility has also accompanied the development of justice, equity, diversity and inclusion agendas (JEDI and variants). With the best of intentions, inclusion has been defined in a manner likely to evoke conservative critiques. The primary focus is upon the under-representation of African American students with a few references to LGBTQ+ communities. Missing from the narrative are, for example, under-represented regions of the USA, military colleges, Christian institutions, and some disciplines. Dialogues about diversity and justice rarely extend to Islamophobia. Jews are more or less missing despite increases in anti-Semitism at home and abroad. The paradox is that inclusion is rather exclusive.

Raising consciousness of diversity and justice issues abroad is only of peripheral interest. The persecution of Christians in many parts of the world, discrimination against Roma in Europe, legalized homophobia in Africa, repression of women by extremist Muslim governments, violence against Muslims in India and Myanmar: these topics are rarely part of the discourse.

A narrow focus on race undermines the principle of inclusion and has given opportunities for reactionary politicians and allies to denigrate and attempt to close JEDI initiatives. Had the principle of inclusion been applied more widely, progressive efforts would have been less vulnerable to those assaults. Critiques of JEDI agendas are symptomatic of widespread challenges facing international education. Political environments are marked by the growth of parochialism and militant nationalism hostile to internationalist ideologies.

The fall of the Berlin Wall in November 1989 was the beginning of events that reshaped Europe and reverberated around the world. The dissolution of the Union of Soviet Socialist Republics followed, and nations re-emerged out of the shadows of the aftermath of World War Two. We celebrated freedom, the lifting of restraints, and liberation. We were not sufficiently aware that older bigotries were also liberated.

We have moved into paradox. We speak of the increasing interdependence of nations, globalization, internationalization, while, simultaneously, historical alienations, xenophobia, and traditional hatreds have created suspicion, isolationism, and disconnection. The contrast between walls and bridges symbolizes a collision between closed and open ideologies.

Hungarian Prime Minister, Viktor Orbán, describes refugees as "Muslim invaders" and "poison", a manifestation of replacement theory that has many adherents in Europe and the USA. The theory posits a global conspiracy to swamp White Christian society with alien intruders, particularly Muslims and Jews. There is an echo here of *The Protocols of the Elders of Zion*, first published in 1903 in Russia. It is an anti-Semitic forgery that describes a secret plot in which a mysterious group of elders plan for Jewish dominance of the world. *The Protocols* is the most persistent and notorious example of the Jewish world-domination conspiracy theory.

In his attack on the Central European University in Budapest, Orbán used traditional anti-Semitic tropes to demonize the founder, George Soros, ultimately forcing the university to relocate to Vienna. Things look good for the far right in much of Europe. Closed ideologies threaten cosmopolitan values across the world.

History reveals a dark road from prejudice through discrimination to persecution. Buried bigotry has moved, in many contexts, from private thought towards legitimized public discourse, and, in extreme cases, government policies. Outsiders are a threat to community security and identity. Racial, ethnic, and religious minorities are increasingly vulnerable. For centuries foreigners were blamed for the spread of disease. Jews and Roma, for example, were unhygienic, carriers of plague. The Great Influenza of 1918 was popularly known as "Spanish flu". The "Chinese virus" and the "Indian variant" marked the beginning of the COVID pandemic. The Nazis refined the notion of racial hygiene. Ethnic cleansing is not only a metaphor but a genocidal objective. In 1936, the Nazis established the Racial Hygiene and Demographic Biology Unit to implement Heinrich Himmler's decree: *Bekampfung der Zigeunerplage* (Combating the Gypsy Plague). Strangers are a problem requiring a solution.

The politics of hate is in direct collision with the ideologies of international education. We are, like it or not, in the business of politics.

Beyond 2023: Reading Tea Leaves

Defenseless under the night
Our world in stupor lies;
Yet, dotted everywhere,
Ironic points of light
Flash out wherever the Just
Exchange their messages
W.H. Auden, *September 1, 1939*

Predicting the future in these perilous times is a complex process in which hope, and fear gnaw away at the consciousness. However, I do not want to conclude, like Jeremiah, by howling at the moon. Despite some of these gloom-laden thoughts, I am, like most educators, mostly optimistic. I have conditional faith in the notion that students can and do move along a spectrum towards relative enlightenment. So, peering at the tea leaves or gazing at the opaque crystal ball, what might we dimly perceive? Despite dark political clouds, we might have faith in the inexorable curiosity of the young that will not be restrained by real or metaphorical borders. Mobility of mind and body is an aspiration of thoughtful humanity across the world.

The barriers are, of course, many. Within the USA, inequality of opportunity is a familiar problem. Across the world, those inequalities are manifestly increased. Between the empowered and the disenfranchised there exists a chasm.

Furthermore, environmentalists seek to discourage mobility. However justified that position is, we need to place responsibility where it primarily belongs – with the producer rather than the consumer. An imperative is the development of cleaner fuels. What, in any case, is the cost to the world of discouraging mobility?

If young people remain within the confines of home, parochial assumptions will be reinforced, that which is foreign will remain alien. Mark Twain's observations are, as so often, imbued with wisdom:

> Travel is fatal to prejudice, bigotry, and narrow-mindedness, and many of our people need it sorely on these accounts. Broad, wholesome, charitable views of men and things cannot be acquired by vegetating in one little corner of the earth.. (1911, p. 407).

Somewhere between 5 and 6 million students study in a country other than their own each year. There are many motivations, of course, but a curiosity about others, a desire to encounter the new, is an impulse that cannot be denied.

In the enveloping gloom, there are points of light.

Pontification of elders will not define the future. This will be made in the minds and hearts of the next generation who, I believe, will cross the boundaries we have built, between countries, and between person and person, mind and mind, soul and soul.

I know many young people, including my own children and colleagues, who retain faith in the power of internationalist ideologies and eschew ideologies of hate. Their dreams, ideals and values offer some optimism for what lies ahead for humanity.

They may yet realize those aspirations that have driven our efforts but remained elusive. These are the tenets of this faith: domestic education can be enhanced by education abroad. The lives of students will be enriched, in many ways, by engagement with new ideas in unfamiliar environments. Encounters with strangers may empower students to cross the most difficult of all borders, that which separates the self from others.

They may teach us that knowledge is not constrained by national boundaries. We may learn the profound truth that no country has a monopoly on wisdom.

REFERENCES

Ashcroft, B., Griffiths, G., & Tiffin, H. (Eds). (2005). *The post-colonial studies reader.* Routledge.

British Academy. (2020). *Qualified for the future.* https://www.thebritishacademy.ac.uk/publications/skills-qualified-future-quantifying-demand-arts-humanities-social-science/

DeParle, J. (2012, January 4). Harder for Americans to rise from lower rungs. *The New York Times.* https://www.nytimes.com/2012/01/05/us/harder-for-americans-to-rise-from-lower-rungs.html

Fulbright, J.W. (1989). *The price of empire.* Pantheon Books.

Pushkar. (2023, April 27). Supply but is there demand? Cites the India skills report. *Times Higher Education.*

Twain, M. (1911). *The innocents abroad,* in *the complete works of Mark Twain.* Harper and Brothers.

Author Bio

Michael Woolf is the Deputy President for Strategic Development at CEACAPA. Mike earned a Ph.D. in American Studies, and he has taught literature at the universities of Hull, Middlesex, Padova, and Venice, and worked as a researcher-writer for the BBC radio. He has held leadership roles in international education for many years and has written widely on professional and academic issues. Additionally, he served on the Board of Directors of the Forum on Education Abroad from 2006 to 2012. He was the recipient of the Forum's 2020 Wollitzer Award. Mike serves as the senior editor of the CEA CAPA Occasional Publications series. A selection of his short essays can be accessed here via this link: https://capaworld.capa.org/silencing-dissent. Email: mwoolf@ceacapa.com

Chapter 6

Reflections on Changing Narratives Supporting Education Abroad

Heidi Soneson
Affiliate, Gateway International Group, United States

Martin Tillman
President, Global Career Compass, United States

ABSTRACT

Two international education veterans reflect on changes in the field of education abroad and student learning over the past forty years. The first perspective examines how the narrative supporting education abroad has shifted from its instrumental value to higher education institutions, focusing instead on student learning outcomes and employability. The second perspective traces a path within institutions of higher education. These two perspectives provide complementary views on how institutions and professionals have adapted to domestic and global challenges and successfully re-aligned the goals of education abroad programs to meet new student needs and academic priorities.

Keywords: Education Abroad, Student Learning, Gen Z, Student Needs, Employment, Careers Aspirations

A Bird's Eye View by Martin Tillman

When I launched my international education career in 1976, I joined a pioneering nonprofit organization called The Lisle Fellowship. No one in my generation of young NAFSA professionals had heard of Lisle; no one was aware of the impact of its pioneering approach to cross-cultural experiential learning. Lisle's summer six-week intercultural educational program was exceptional; for decades, it was the only opportunity for either American or international students to have deep interaction with each other in a structured experiential learning environment off campus.

In the decades prior to the establishment of NAFSA in 1948, the launching of the Fulbright program, and the post-WWII expansion of U.S. higher education, there were few – if any – off campus domestic or international intercultural learning programs intentionally fostering interaction with either international or domestic college students. There was scant attention to co-curricular domestic off-campus programs. This was the face of the emerging field of international education after the end of WWII and the context in which the profession operated.

Thus, my career began with an acute awareness of the historical limitations of traditional campus efforts to connect large numbers of students to the wider world through study abroad or international service-learning (excluding the Peace Corps). The status quo was not challenged in this period. This was not the fault of administrators; the failure lay in the systemic constraints of the higher education system.

I traveled the country to promote Lisle programs on campuses. Similarly, other off-campus organizations, like the Experiment in International Living (aka World Learning), had individuals traveling to directly discuss their programs with campus staff and students. International offices were small and often posted brochures mailed to them on bulletin boards in hallways. Safe to say, the absence of any formal means of advertising or structured marketing kept the opportunities for education abroad from being widely known except to relatively small cohorts of highly motivated students on a selective number of campuses conducting study abroad programs (often led by faculty with scholarly ties to countries in their discipline).

Over time, we can trace the gradual professionalization of the field of international education to the growth of resources and stature of NAFSA. Between 1950-75, NAFSA developed its first "professional sections" and collaborated with a wider cross-section of campus personnel and community volunteers. The Section on US Students Studying Abroad was created. For the first time, significant support came from the State Department's Bureau of Education and Cultural Affairs; these funds launched a wide range of training and professional development initiatives. And the private sector, especially the

Ford Foundation, stepped in with funding for NAFSA and the Institute for International Education.

As the post-war U.S. and world economy strengthened, and the organizational and campus infrastructure supporting student mobility grew and matured, we witnessed a slow rise in the numbers of U.S. students studying abroad and international students entering the U.S. Despite greater attention in the 1960s and 1970s to sending more students to study abroad, there was insufficient examination of how the structure and design of the programs themselves would impact the students' overall learning experience and attainment of specific learning outcomes. Campuses focused their attention on the instrumental aspects of administration of education abroad and less on the motivation of the student, their expectations, and the role of other student affairs offices in assisting students prepare for their journey abroad.

As the field matured in the 1980s and 1990s, economic globalization and expansion of institutional practices and policies that would impact internationalization, forced campuses and provider organizations to respond to new questions. There was a new stress on the extrinsic value of education abroad. How should campuses more intentionally prepare students to succeed in the global economy? How should campuses prepare students to successfully transition into an expanding global economy? What new options were opening to align emerging campus international education priorities and practices with the needs of a wider global workforce?

Since the early 2000s, I witnessed a steady evolution of support for the proposition that international experience could, if purposefully designed in tandem with a holistic student advising practice, meaningfully contribute to both student career development and post-graduation employability. A new narrative supporting campus internationalization was emerging: *Education abroad linked to employability outcomes could achieve gains in competencies that add value to student career decision- making and postgraduate job searches.*

It is important to note that employability is not synonymous with employment; the two are often confused as meaning the same thing. Employability is the accumulation of skills and competencies through applied experiences both at home and abroad, inside and outside the classroom and in the community. Employment is the "condition of having paid work" in a trade or profession. To succeed at the latter, a student must first successfully build a portfolio of employable skill sets and credentials which are of value to a particular employer in a given sector of the economy.

My early research (2014) showed there were few campuses with integrated student advising practices specifically tied to the design of education abroad programs. In other words, career service offices were not in any way purposefully supporting students, either before they left the US, or upon their return home. Of course, there were noteworthy exceptions: Michigan State University, University of Michigan and University of Minnesota successfully engaged their faculty and student affairs staff to create exemplary career integration models.

I've also tracked – along with a growing number of colleagues in Australia, the Netherlands, Finland, Italy, and England – the increasing importance of building effective partnerships with employers. Looking back, the academic community never saw a need to view employers as allies in their internationalization practices. However, both geo-political currents and economic pressures created pressure for new partnerships with employers in all sectors.

In one of the earliest pieces of research demonstrating the convergence of interests between academic institutions and employers (2012), I stated, "University policymakers and administrators need to take a fresh look at the design and structure of international education programs if these experiences are intended to have a maximum impact on the career direction and near and long-term employability of students."

Tacking to the increasing availability of a wide range of international- and domestic-internships which developed as momentum for employer partnerships picked up steam, we've seen further expansion of both internships (hybrid and in-person) and virtual study abroad as a direct result of the pandemic these last three years. I believe that a silver-lining from the Covid lockdown period is that campuses and organizations, forced to adapt and take risks with the technology, found an innovative pathway via Zoom to bring these co-curricular experiences to the attention of new and more diverse cohorts of students. Students who otherwise would not have had the exposure to these types of experiential learning.

Going forward, we need new research to examine and assess how students benefited from virtual learning and similarly, how employers and faculty view how successful the learning outcomes proved to be for their classroom and workplace needs.

In coming years, as students, faculty, program administrators and organizational leaders settle further into a new "post-" Covid normal, I would hope to see greater time and resources applied in these areas:

- Cross-training of career counselors and international office program staff

- Increased dialogue with faculty about the value added by linking education abroad (both virtual and in-person) with employability
- Greater engagement with employers to assess their needs for talent and their perspective on the career-readiness of students
- Development of a wider range of strategies for career integration processes to assist students in making informed decisions about the type of education abroad experience best aligned to support their academic program and career aspirations

A View from the Kaleidoscope by Heidi Soneson

My journey spans more than four decades of education abroad experiences – as a college student studying abroad in London for an academic year and then as a volunteer in Kenya, as a graduate student studying in Germany, as a study abroad advisor, a program director, and ultimately as Assistant Vice Chancellor for International Education. Viewing the field and its trajectory from both inside the looking glass and then as an advisor and leader facilitating opportunities for students in higher education, the changes have been profound.

The students I encountered in my early years as a study abroad advisor in the 1980's mirrored, in many ways, my own college study abroad experience a number of years earlier. Students often chose the option to study at a university abroad, took liberal arts courses, and received credit towards graduation and possibly for their major or minor as well. Alternatively, unique experiences focused on cultural engagement at non-traditional locations attracted the more adventurous students. The interest was the cultural experience with an understanding that credit transfer would typically apply broadly rather than specifically for major or minor requirements. It was not unusual for students to let me know that credit was important, but an interesting cultural experience was the source of their excitement. Location mattered, and students would often share with me the location that they had always wanted to visit as the motivation for their program selection. Opportunities for students with limited flexibility in their coursework was challenging unless the students were satisfied with fulfilling liberal education requirements or general credits towards graduation. This era, for those who could afford both the time and cost to go abroad, offered a rich array of cultural experiences at both traditional and non-traditional locations. It also required a comfort level with ambiguity, as many students relied on the overseas infrastructure and integrated fully into the overseas university environment.

My career move to a program director position and at a new institution in the early 1990's accompanied a shift in focus for the education abroad field as well. Faculty-led short-term programs provided field-specific overseas opportunities, thereby expanding the range of academic opportunities for students and the range of students who would elect to study abroad. University courses abroad remained the primary focus for longer term experiences, but there was increasing interest in identifying and hiring consistent support staff to ensure continuity and provide stability for faculty leaders and students. Resident directors and specialized courses for the U.S. provided a critical framework to expand student access. U.S. faculty increasingly asked for more detailed information on courses offered abroad in order to identify course equivalencies for their students. Student access and curricular alignment, along with a growing emphasis on standards for risk management, heralded a new and expanding commitment to education abroad among faculty, administration, and students.

The ground-breaking initiative known as curriculum integration initiated a structured approach to matching overseas coursework with U.S. courses across university departments. This undertaking, which now seems so self-evident, highlighted the importance of identifying coursework abroad – whether at an overseas university or through specialized courses – for a broader student audience. Student interest, encouraged by their faculty advisors, shifted as well. Students might still come to the education abroad office with one or more locations in mind, but the importance of identifying locations that would offer the courses students needed for their major and/or minor credit received equal if not more attention and focus, and education abroad offices along with education abroad providers and overseas staff developed advising materials that focused on curricular match and alignment.

A greater emphasis on clarifying the relationship between education abroad and career planning for students further increased interest in studying abroad. Human Resource directors at companies who once stated that studying abroad was a nice enhancement to a student's resume were now indicating that an applicant wouldn't even be in the first selection group unless a study abroad experience was listed.

In addition, initiatives to support diverse student identities (students with disabilities, students of color, first-generation students, to name just a few) reinforced the importance of individual student interests, needs, and focus. The time period through the mid 2000's was an exciting time of expansion at an exponential rate for education abroad.

Technology advancement certainly fueled this growth in many ways. Where, at a time in the past, a parent would tell me that a certain country was "too far away" for their student to study because there was only the option of postal correspondence, telex, or the long journey to make a visit to that country, the advent of Facebook, cell phones, texting, and email bridged distances psychologically for both students and parents, and enabled prompt communication between education abroad offices and overseas sites.

It is important to state, of course, that world events did not always allow for smooth sailing. The Persian Gulf War, SARS, MERS, Ebola all had significant impact on education programs in areas most affected by these world conditions and resulted in tense moments of both group and individual student evacuations, program suspensions, and close coordination with overseas program directors and university colleagues to design and implement responsive health and safety protocols that laid the foundation for the essential and expanding role of international health and safety experts in education abroad offices.

There is no doubt that the era of expansive growth and diversification in education abroad came to a shocking and sudden pause with the world-wide impact of COVID-19. It is quite possible, and perhaps even likely, that "business as usual" will not return because the world has changed. COVID-19 is now part of our daily lives with no specific end in sight. Russia's war with the Ukraine has an impact far beyond two nations, and China's expansion into Hong Kong and a looming threat towards Taiwan has reshaped education abroad options and required cautious planning for unanticipated realities. In spite of these challenges, or perhaps because of them, a number of unique future directions are materializing:

- Virtual learning provides access to and support for international learning in innovative ways. A number of organizations, for example, now have as their specific focus the opportunity for students to gain job-specific experiences and skills through virtual internships with companies abroad. This not only enhances the relationship between international learning and professional skills, it expands the student audience that can benefit from this kind of international learning.

- Virtual modules have the ability to integrate international experiences into U.S. university classrooms. As a German language teacher many years ago, I would share my enthusiasm for German and international experiences with my university students. Now instructors can bring that world into the classroom and even engage students in live conversations with individuals abroad. This can occur in a wide range of academic fields – from biology to business to engineering.

- COIL continues to build bridges across academic departments, faculty, and students internationally and reinforces the importance of collaborative problem-solving across borders. Education abroad is no longer only an experience overseas; it can and should be part of every student's education in the classroom.

- Health and safety protocols will continue to be a critical emphasis with greater uniformity of standards across U.S. institutions. The recent advocacy by NAFSA and the Forum with the U.S. Department of State regarding the U.S. Department of State Travel Advisories is just one example of the growing importance of health and safety standards that take into consideration guidance for education abroad.

- The importance of creating and sustaining programs that can meet diverse student needs in a well-structured, well-supported environment abroad is now paramount. This opens the door to develop programs for a wide range of student audiences by building on established infrastructure abroad. This can include both short- and long-term opportunities, professional skills-focused internships, and short-term volunteer experiences. Engaging learning centers and on-site organizations at diverse locations across the globe, including access to overseas universities, will realize a unique and rich portfolio for students from across the curriculum.

CONCLUSION

Many U.S. institutions are maximizing this "reset" period to assess their current structures and consider leading practices. Identifying sustaining fiscal policies, strategic program expansion, and essential staffing needs are important considerations to prepare for the steady and renewed interest in education abroad among U.S. students. There is also a unique opportunity to collaborate across institutional offices and departments in order to build comprehensive learning opportunities for students. Consultation and collaboration with career offices and diversity and equity offices on campus, for example, are essential pillars for education abroad sustainability.

Education abroad will also need to address the emerging reality of the non-career world that young adults are entering. There is much discussion that current college graduates will move into a "project-based" professional world and hold multiple jobs over the course of their adult lives. A number of high school graduates also chose to delay starting their college education due to the impact of the COVID-19 pandemic. What kind of learning should course offerings abroad incorporate for this next generation? Perhaps topics such as reducing our carbon footprint, identifying alternative energy sources, developing specific skills to function successfully in multiple cultural environments, and identifying strategies for engaging effectively with diverse constituents can be incorporated successfully into virtual or in-person education abroad courses and can create the building blocks for our future generations.

We are still in the process of learning from and adapting to the world as we now find it. Hopefully, discussions will continue to take place in journals, at conferences, and on campuses regarding the future we can and should realize together.

REFERENCES

Kumar, V. S. (2023, April 18). *Gen Z in the workplace: How should companies adapt?* https://imagine.jhu.edu.

Prakash, P. (2023, June 24). *Gen Z workers came of age amid the pandemic – and now quitting their job is always front of mind.* http://fortune.com.

Smith, M. (2023, January 18). *Gen Z and millennials are leading 'the big quit' in 2023 – why nearly 70% plan to leave their jobs.* CNBC. https://CNBC.com.

Tillman, M. (2014). *Campus best practices supporting education abroad & student career development,* American Institute for Foreign Study.

Tillman, M. (2012). Employer perspectives on international education. In D. Deardorff, H. de Witt, J. Heyl, & T. Adams (Eds.), *The SAGE handbook of international higher education* (pp.191-206). Sage Publications, Inc.

Author Bios

Martin Tillman, M.A., is former Associate Director of Career Services at the

Johns Hopkins University Paul Nitze School of Advanced International Studies (ret.). He is an Affiliate of the Gateway International Group and Consultant/Trainer for GlobalEd. He has published widely and his research focuses on global workforce trends and the impact of education abroad on student career development and employability. His Global Career Compass blog is widely read. Email: martyjtillman@gmail.com.

Heidi Soneson, Ph.D., is an Affiliate of the Gateway International Group and has held positions as Executive Director of the Office of International Education and Assistant Vice Chancellor for International Education at the University of Wisconsin – River Falls as well as Program Director in the Learning Abroad Center at the University of Minnesota, among other positions. Dr. Soneson has published and presented on a variety of study abroad topics, including student experiences and colonial legacy, study abroad for students with disabilities, visa regulations for US students, ethical visa advising guidelines, GLBT concerns, study abroad in non-traditional locations, and strategies for raising the visibility of study abroad offices on U.S. campuses. Email: hsoneson@comcast.net.

Chapter 7

Walls and Doors, To Each Their Time

Joshua S. McKeown, Ph.D.
Associate Provost for International Education at SUNY Oswego,
International Education Leadership Fellow, the University at Albany

ABSTRACT

America's contradictory tendencies towards isolationism and global engagement appear and reappear as predictably as a swinging pendulum. International educators who bask in heady times of growth must navigate lean times in creative and sometimes cunning ways to protect what we have built. Prior to the global pandemic in 2020, education abroad and international student mobility grew to unprecedented levels of expansion, diversity, and sophistication, only for it all to be halted in its tracks. As the world and our profession emerge from this disruptive experience, it is time to take stock of where we fit into the larger higher education landscape and provide lessons and perspective to the next generation inheriting our cause and dedication. Specific recommendations include: taking action within contexts of engagement and isolation, knowing the limits of our professional roles, reconciling faltering expectations of our students and institutions, and accepting the rewards and compromises of an international life and career.

Keywords: Education Abroad, International Education, Student Engagement, Study Abroad, Student Development, Senior International Officer, International Education Leadership

Never fear. We may let the scaffolds fall
Confident that we have built our wall.

from "Scaffolding" by Seamus Heaney

America has a stubborn, predictable habit of turning inwards, only to be shocked into needing to engage with the world again. We are the ones who keep it going.

Writing today, barely removed from a global pandemic, watching authoritarians and nationalists build walls of steel, technology, and ignorance in seemingly every direction, one could be soured on the whole thing. But we have been here before.

Growing up and starting to understand life a bit in the 1970s and 80s near the end of the Cold War, it was understood that there were places in the world that one couldn't go, or wouldn't go. After the horrible wall in Berlin was torn down, within a dozen years or so things swung wildly. I helped my institution develop programs abroad that a few years before would have been unimaginable. We ran programs in trauma studies to earthquake-struck Haiti, in gender studies researching human trafficking to India, in social justice education to sub-Saharan Africa, and when earnest students wanted to assist refugees in war torn Darfur, Sudan - we considered it seriously. Yet another dozen years later I was canceling programs and evacuating hundreds of students in the face of a global pandemic that no one in our field had experienced before. We were told by government leaders that sealing borders and preventing mobility was a logical and necessary process to which we had to obey, as if it were clear and obvious that a wall could surround us and protect us from everything. The pendulum swings.

Reflecting on a 30-year career in international higher education is humbling, at least it is for me. To be viewed as a leader when, really, I feel like a survivor reminds me, like the Seamus Heaney poem, to remember the scaffolding even while focusing on our earnest wall. The *how* we do what we do as international educators, our disposition, our relentless passion towards opening doors especially to young people who need worthy guides when craven wall builders and carnival barkers entice them with easy escapes and scapegoats.

But let us remember the right and good meaning of a wall. A wall, like the sturdy one turned to while going to sleep snuggly in a grandparent's home, is one of safety. A wall, where a kid plays ball with friends at school recess, builds confidence. A wall, remembering fallen heroes on the National Mall in DC or murals of meaning in Anytown, USA, gives us historic stability and civic recognition, an enduring edifice to what we mean to ourselves and others. A wall we lean our heads against to rest with effort made, with steadfastness of purpose in our work that welcomes newcomers to safety and encourages voyagers to remember as they look over their shoulders, is one we can count on. But we know that those are not the only walls imagined around us.

Chimeras of Success

The sureness with which higher education and broader US society embraced international education during times of plentiful priority has typically revealed our next limitations. Like the hopeful, exhaling period following the Cold War, after many lifetimes of hardship, violence, and endurance were spent on seemingly nothing, or during the hyper-globalist years after 9/11 but before the financial crisis when *The New York Times* declared it "the study-abroad generation" (2007). A few years after each we quickly took our back seat when told. Memories of the strain of the international educator after the evocative shock of the bombing of flight Pan Am 103 in 1988, or during the arduous years of the global pandemic, I think should bring balance to even the most accomplished Senior International Officer, to render us less sanguine and evangelistic, perhaps more reasonable about what success really is and more respectful of the places and people who will never understand what we hold dear, let alone join in our exuberance.

Assurances in the moment can lead the rookie or the forgetful to feel all-too-much at the center of things; then terrorists or Wall Street or bludgeoning heads of state remind us that we are only the door-keepers. Not door-makers or door-judges, not even door-designers or -deciders, only keepers of the watch. We prefer to be forever opening them wider, but that is not always possible. The more I go on, the more I appreciate a decent if restrained role, picking my battles carefully to ensure the whole international education enterprise keeps going. It is ours and if we don't maintain it no one else will.

We need to have decorum. We must move subtly when needed and be subversive in the right ways when necessary, and to keep our eyes on the prize even if at times we disappoint ourselves when we know more could be possible in the moment. We know, or we should, that we could easily be crushed by the mob *du jour* for our openness and willingness to engage with the other, the foreign, and for our lack of absolutism. If we are trained well, we find a way to maintain communication and exchange mechanisms even when their existence demands to be shut down by power, because if they succeed it is possible those relations will never restart.

We are the ones who keep it going.

Remember Which Era You're In

As a matter of survival, I would suggest to the practitioner to determine in which of two broad categories of eras you exist: are you in an expansive, maybe even heroic, era of actively crossing borders and assertively opening doors? Or more so in a time of caution and tidying things up, lest we do the wrong thing and bring about any sort of financial, legal, or personnel scrutiny? Principles aside, I believe that the macro question of era matters greatly. If we find ourselves in the former place we can take more chances, being accountable and responsible but accepting more risks because we are encouraged to invite more possibilities. Note how much US education abroad diversified its destinations, student participants, and program models during expansive periods, as well as unprecedented growth in international student enrollment (Institute of International Education).

But if we find ourselves in a less open, more restrictive or isolationist time, regardless of the impetus, such as what may be coming into view now as something of a *lost generation of globalization*, we need to take stock. In which ways does our work reflect our institution's strategic priorities, specifically? I think we should be able to name three clear ones and carry them around in our heads at all times. In which ways do the rewards of our work, namely helping people cross borders for educational purposes, justify the potential risks? The programs we design and deliver are high-impact practices with clear ties to student development (McKeown et. al, 2021), retention (Ogden et. al, 2023), and career success (Farugia & Sanger, 2017). We need to regularly articulate and remind others of what we do and how impactful it is. In which ways does our work support, or go against, what our state or federal government expects of us? If you had to explain what went wrong, to your president, the state legislature, or a probing reporter, who is by your side?

As a roadmap towards a future iteration of our profession, I would offer the following themes as ones to think about for yourself first before getting to the specific plans and strategies you must later. What do you see happening with your students and your institutional situation? Let it guide your actions.

Assessing Risk Within the Individual Not Just the Location

"Get yourselves lost" was literally what a study abroad director told me and a group of fellow undergraduates given a free afternoon in a strange city we had never visited before. *Get yourselves lost.* I took it to mean that we should explore, meet the unknown, confront our fears, and figure out how to get back. We did, without GPS or mobile phones in our pockets either. That was nearly 35 years ago.

Not everyone can do that and not every generation is the same. The level of mental health concern today is high relative to previous years (Spiner, 2022) and in particular for underrepresented students for whom utilization of mental health services is known to be lower (Lipson et. al, 2022, pp. 138-147). Education abroad students' comfort level with uncertainty may be significantly lower than before the pandemic (Harder & Mullaney, 2021; McKeown & Bergman-Ray, 2023, pp. 853-874). As future crises hit, advising students to go off the grid by themselves without a plan versus a more prescribed and less risk-averse approach might work, but I would advise taking stock of the moment as you design and deliver programs, regardless the location, to make sure your students and institution would actually benefit from this more than the risk it could bring to you.

What may be lost in this exchange of assurance and certainty for less risk is the magic of discovery. Risk management is not usually discussed alongside serendipity. But be open to when you can encourage them to go out of their comfort zones, just be careful the moment allows it and that your decision is supported. The pendulum will surely swing back at some point. We must live to fight another day.

Reconciling the Issue of Student Expectations and Demands

Genuine concerns have been raised by the best in our profession (Castiello-Gutiérrez & Gozik, 2022) about education abroad perpetuating imbalances in power and privilege. I have argued previously (McKeown, 2009) that getting young Americans abroad, especially for the first time, in deliberately designed academic programs will benefit them significantly. Others have argued that education abroad opens up greater possible definitions of global citizenship (Ogden, 2010). All of this resides within the unfortunate legacy in America of minimal participation in education abroad despite the massive potential developmental, academic, and career impacts cited above.

Giving our students what they want as customers is tempting but also problematic; so is, in my view, insisting that they learn only the most pure and profound version of international education that we can muster. As a roadmap for the future of our profession, this topic should give us pause. While the idea of a "study-abroad generation" may now be passé, the YouTube generation or the TikTok generation may not always be interested in or ready for our best educational intentions. Most of us, I suspect, will not be satisfied that we have done our jobs just by delivering students to a spot where they take a selfie and post it on social media, but we might want to start to acknowledge that visions of experiences like those may be what drew students to our programs in the first place. There lies our opportunity.

Any of us who have walked into a classroom recently and seen our students all on their phones, not talking to each other, not making friends or potential life or business partners with those sitting next to them, may wonder where this generation is going to end up. I believe that our profession will continue to do its duty if we make our programs appealing yet at times uncomfortable for students, but not unmanageable; something that used to be called *challenge and support* (Sanford, 1966). While I believe we should not list our program components like amenities on a luxury cruise (unless we are prepared to hire a concierge to ensure that type of experience), we need to be aware that anxieties over things like housing placement and how travel will proceed are real and may prevent students from going abroad with us if we cannot see it from their perspective.

Since education abroad is, at all but the most elite institutions, an optional and expensive student choice, if they choose not to go abroad with us then we as international educators will have lost the opportunity to educate them and show them the world. I am inclined to let them take their selfies, post their moments on social media to friends back home, and call their parents if they want to. I do this knowing that they are learning something extraordinary while abroad, and probably making great new friends and forming new personal relationships at the same time as experiencing something authentic and powerful on my programs because I designed them that way. If I need to promote this as a fun experience in order for them to go, I will.

Dealing with Larger Questions of Educational Purpose

At my undergraduate institution, which was one of the largest and best education abroad providers in the United States, there were exactly four program choices: England, France, Italy, and Spain. That was a long time ago. Those places were then and are now all great program sites worth visiting, but not exactly what the industry came to see as a robust and proper program portfolio over the ensuing decades. Up until the recent pandemic, my considerably humbler institution had over 80 active programs in more than 30 countries on all continents of the world except Antarctica (and we were working on that).

Had I been in the position to ask the study abroad director or chancellor of my undergraduate university why there were only four choices, they might have said something like what I am starting to hear now and see around our profession today: it was what was possible and realistic, it was where students and parents felt safe going, it was where payments could be made and infrastructure could be identified and health care systems were comparable, etc., etc. I admit I have had to make similar determinations since the end of the pandemic; some of my long standing programs are still formally suspended.

But let us not assume that large European cities were magical utopias of wonder and luxury in those days either. We learned in Madrid through the frequency of terrorist bombs what aggrieved ethnic minorities were capable of after decades of repression. Friends studying in London came face to face with the violence of The Troubles in real life, not just their TV screens, and perhaps reconsidered their own biases and assumptions. And colonial legacies and racial inequalities in Paris and across the European continent were becoming impossible to ignore for all but the most myopic traveler.

The point then as now is that there are powerful, provocative, and daunting situations that students can learn from even in seemingly harmonious and comfortable places. Identifying what you want students to learn should drive this process. It may be again that parts of the world are, or soon will be, unwise to travel to, or our students will tell us which locations are not viable because they stop applying to go to them. Studying and learning about the entire world is still possible, but it may need to be more modestly designed in times like these. Or as a great international educator once told me, "less is more" (W. Melczer, personal communication, 1990).

Managing Expectations and Explaining Deficiencies

As leaders we do not have the luxury of only thinking and writing. We have departments and divisions to lead, staff to manage, colleagues to motivate, and stakeholders to inform. The amount of effort, ambiguity, and friction in international education lately speaks to the headwinds many in our field face. Again, we have been here before, but recognizing the regulatory, financial, political, and geopolitical constraints on our work must be done. The extent to which we take on risks, identify which staff expertise to seek, and ultimately decide which programs to design and run depend on this.

The expectations of staff and faculty colleagues can shift. It might start with little things, like a young staff person deciding she would rather decline a travel opportunity because of your office politics or the institution's red tape. It could be when a strong performer tells you they are resigning, maybe leaving higher education entirely, due to the dueling bureaucracy and other deficiencies of universities as organizations that was keeping them up at night and ultimately wasn't worth it. Or maybe it is when a veteran faculty program leader decides he no longer wants to lead students abroad, and you learn quietly that he had a panic attack at the airport and cannot do this anymore.

The great thing about institutions of higher education is that they are populated with smart people and within them everything is theoretically possible. The reality for most of us who survive an entire career is that they are loosely coupled, politicized institutions skimpy on resources for pretty much everyone. Yet we true believers in international education put up with it because the impact on the next generations is so powerful and our intrinsic rewards so great.

Looking back on my career and helping assemble this roadmap to the future of our profession, I would recommend to all to pay much closer attention to the real ways that your institutions are organized. Not the niceties of official publications, statements of mission, vision, or values, rather, focus more on the mechanical things and operational processes. How are people hired and trained? How are people incentivized and promoted? Who pays which bills, and how clear is that approval process? What does faculty governance do, when is it required, and in what ways is it bypassed? Who deals with the media, the state and federal governments, and how much access to the president's office do students, parents, alumni, and staff like you have? We have control and sometimes influence over some of these matters, I recommend identifying them.

Designing and sustaining a robust international offering is hard, we do not and cannot follow many normal campus policies and procedures; the things we buy are not like ordering computers or copy paper. Regardless of our beliefs and values as international educators, we will not get anything done unless we correctly gauge and perform within these operational scenarios. We have to harmonize the regulatory expectations of rigid and resource-poor institutions with the ambitions of our own professional enterprise and students' worldly dreams. We must mitigate between agonizing legal risks and life-changing, joyful experiences for our brightest young people. Looking back, I accept the times when a prudent half-full glass was what we drank from, but only so as to maintain us, solidify us, protect and later propel us forward. Never because we were fearful.

Small steps are ok if that's all that's possible. We are the ones who keep it going.

Conclusion

Authentic experience is still sought. Whether examined in a doctoral dissertation or displayed in an admissions brochure, education abroad continues to be the thing that is the most alluring, the most expansive, the most challenging, and perhaps the most desired single aspect of a university education. But what else would someone like me say?

I had an experience not long ago of a different sort that reminded me of this. I was attending an outdoor community festival with my son. As the days' craft vendors and street performers packed up, a nighttime dance party assembled with competing DJs each playing on color-coded headphones that allowed dancers to choose their genre. Groups formed, people switched to different DJs when it looked like they had a following, break dancers hit the streets. It was wild, it was real, and it was something even a tween kid who had never experienced it before could understand right away, be blown away by, and talk about for days. It wasn't on a cruise ship or at Disney World either. It was on the street. Authenticity matters.

Education abroad takes many forms, but if it doesn't excite and infuse something powerful in our students, as well as inform and educate them for a full life, then we are missing the opportunity. The lack of student engagement post-pandemic that so many in higher education are concerned about, with the accompanying urgency of mental health, enrollment and retention, equity and justice, and environmental sustainability, could very well be helped through these authentic experiences that students yearn for and connect with. Education abroad will always be this. We should better it, protect it, and fight for it. I hope that some of these ideas and considerations, whether bold or understated, help you and at the right time.

I like to conclude my remarks at new student orientations and pre-departure sessions with a story I first read about from China. I have also learned that people from India and elsewhere know the story, and it surely applies to America. It is the story of the frog who lives in a well and, when he looks up, thinks he is seeing the whole sky. Only outside the well can the frog see and experience everything that the world is. I liken international education to this, whether as an American going abroad or an international student coming to the US.

Those students are the ones we have reached. Unfortunately, the metaphorical walls of the well in that story can represent the American isolationist habit. Those walls in that well are surely solid, but not healthy and not revealing the complexity of the whole world; in fact, they are designed to keep it out. But somehow, at least in my version of the story, the frog gets out. It must have climbed the wall, using its sureness and solidity to provide both sound footing and a purposeful path. Maybe it had a good guide or door-keeper.

As international educators we are in a privileged position to help young people choose the wall of confidence that helps them climb up to a higher and better place, to see the whole sky, the whole world. Whether for the first time, or for the hundredth, we should embrace the enduring importance of this experience. Even if the scaffolding eventually falls away, and we ourselves are forgotten, it is worth it.

It is ours. We are the ones who kept it going.

REFERENCES

Castiello-Gutiérrez, S., & Gozik, N. J. (2022). Decolonizing education abroad: Grounding theory in practice. In N. J. Gozik, & H. B. Hamir (Eds), *A house where all belong: Redesigning education abroad for inclusive excellence.* The Forum on Education Abroad. DOI: 10.36366/SIA.1.978-1-952376-21-4.9

Farrugia, C. F., & Sanger, J. (2017). *Gaining an employment edge: The impact of study abroad on 21st century skills & career prospects in the United States.* IIE Center for Academic Mobility Research and Impact. https://www.iie.org/publications/gaining-an-employment-edge-the-impact-of-study-abroad/

Harder, W., & Mullaney, J. L. (2021). *Never getting off the ground or heading home early: Student perceptions and experiences of study abroad disruption during COVID-19.* Routledge. DOI: 10.4324/9781003138402-5.

Institute of International Education. (n.d.). *U.S. Study Abroad.* https://opendoorsdata.org/data/us-study-abroad/

Lipson, S. K., Zhou, S., Abelson, S., Heinze, J., Jirsa, M., Morigney, J., Patterson, A., Singh, M., & Eisenberg, D. (2022). Trends in college student mental health and help-seeking by race/ethnicity: Findings from the national healthy minds study, 2013–2021. *Journal of Affective Disorders, 306,* 138-137.https://doi.org/10.1016/j.jad.2022.03.038.

McKeown, J. S. (2009). *The first time effect:The impact of study abroad on college student intellectual development.* Albany: State University of New York Press.

McKeown, J. S., Celaya, M. L., & Ward, H. H. (2021). Academic development: The impact of education abroad on students as learners. In A. C. Ogden, B. Streitwieser, & C. V. Mol. (Eds.), *Education Abroad: Bridging Scholarship and Practice.* Routledge.

McKeown, J. S., & Bergman-Ray, C. (2023). COVID-19 and US higher education: Impact on student mobility. *Creative Education, 14*. DOI: 10.4236/ce.2023.144056.

Ogden, A. C. (2010). *Education abroad and the making of global citizens: Assessing learning outcomes of course-embedded, faculty-led international programming*. Michigan: Ann Arbor.

Ogden, A. C., Ho, H. Z., Lam, Y. W., Bell, A. D., Bhatt, R., Hodges, L., Shiflet, C., & Rubin, D. (2023). The impact of education abroad participation on college student success among first-generation students. *The Journal of Higher Education*. DOI: 10.1080/00221546.2023.2182569

Sanford, N. (1966). Development through challenge. *Self and society: Social change and individual development.* New York: Atherton.

Spiner, T. (2022). 14 emerging trends: The pandemic era has changed attitudes toward science and mental health. *American Psychological Association, 53* (1).

The New York Times. (2007, September 24). *The study-abroad generation*. The New York Times.
https://archive.nytimes.com/essay.blogs.nytimes.com/2007/09/24/the-study-abroad-generation/?smid=nytcore-ios-share&referringSource=articleShare

Author Bio

Joshua S. McKeown, Ph.D., is the Associate Provost for International Education at SUNY Oswego and International Education Leadership Fellow at the University at Albany. He led SUNY Oswego to awards from American Association of State Colleges & Universities (AASCU), Institute of International Education (IIE), Diversity Abroad, and Chinese Service Center for Scholarly Exchange (CSCSE). McKeown co-edited *Global Higher Education During COVID-19: Policy, Society, and Technology* (STAR Scholars, 2021) and authored the chapter *Coming in from the Cold: US-China Academic Relations After COVID-19*. His publications include *The First Time Effect: The Impact of Study Abroad on College Student Intellectual Development* (SUNY Press 2009), *Wasted Talents? China's Higher Education Reforms Experienced Through Its Visiting Scholars Abroad* (Journal of Contemporary China, 2021), chapters in *Education Abroad: Bridging Scholarship and Practice* (Routledge, 2020) and *NAFSA's Guide to Education Abroad* (NAFSA, 2014). He was a Fulbright-Nehru International Education Administrators recipient for India, a mentor with IIE's Connecting with the World Myanmar program, and has served professional organizations including CEA CAPA, AIRC, and Phi Beta Delta Honor Society for International Scholars. Email: joshua.mckeown@oswego.edu

Chapter 8

Perspectives and Experience in International Education

Insights from a Veteran Educator

Sora H. Friedman
SIT Graduate Institute, United States

ABSTRACT

In this look back at the history and forward to possible trends of the field of international Education, the author reflects on their experiences as an IE professional and related challenges and trends. Challenges include the need to keep pace with constant change, to increase diversity and access to educational mobility programs, and to promote deep personal awareness and global learning of participants in the face of increased attachment to personal technology. Accomplishments include the professionalization of the field through increased rigorous knowledge production such as peer-reviewed research and publications, professional conferences, and the establishment of advanced educational programs. The essay closes with a call to always keep the rationales for our work central to our professional consciousness, to both cherish and grow the joy we feel when learning and self-awareness happen, and to support those in the future who will consider our lived experiences as their histories.

Keywords: Challenges, History, International Education, Skills, Trends

INTRODUCTION

In my first Cultural History course taken as part of my doctoral studies, the professor (who eventually became chair of my dissertation committee), Dr. Lawrence Levine, opened the course by asking why we study history. All of the students in the room quickly responded, almost in unison, with the common adage that those who do not study history are doomed to repeat it. Larry scoffed at us while first smiling and then rejecting that easy answer. He then started to pose questions about context, stakeholders, changes, values, roles, power, etc., and we began to understand that the reason to study history was not to avoid repeating it (some of it is unavoidable and some of it is also pretty positive) but instead, to understand where we come from, how we ended up where we are at this time, and how what has passed might affect our futures.

Reflecting on this lesson from one of my most respected teachers and mentors, the consideration of the history of the field of International Education is even more interesting to me. There is much to be learned from our history, and of course, there are as many histories as there are professionals, students, programs, and institutions, as we each have our own stories to share and learn from.

ENTERING THE FIELD

I started working in the field of international education in the early 1980s, after a few years of student-level experiences and before I even knew it was a field! I first volunteered with exchange students in high school and then worked in my undergraduate study abroad office for three years. Little did I know that with those experiences, I was laying the foundation for an amazing career. What I did know is that after being a high school exchange student to Bolivia and spending my junior year of college in Colombia, I loved spending time with people from different places, I was drawn to helping create and run programs that celebrated culture, and (once I started graduate school at SIT) learning about intercultural theory felt both magical and validating. Very few people I knew understood the world of international education as a profession or discipline, and so, my path was quite accidental. Upon graduation, I worked as a secretary with the U.S. Department of State while volunteering with AFS Intercultural Programs. After about eight months, a staff position opened at AFS and I realized that I could get paid to do what I did as a volunteer. It was a "light bulb moment" when what I thought was something that would remain on the periphery of my career turned out to be part of a larger professional community and little by little, I learned that I could have a career in exchange program management. The field of International Education has been my professional home, truly a part of my identity, ever since.

While the motivations of today's IE professionals are similar to those of us who started 30 and 40 years ago, the milieu in which we studied and worked then were quite different. In the 1980s, it was impossible to earn a master's degree in international education. Instead, one could only study related fields such as language and area studies, communications, political science, and international administration. No one told you about developing a career in IE; you found it by happenstance. And of course, resources were very different. The work was conducted with paper and telephones and mimeograph machines, and what can now take seconds at our fingertips, back then involved countless hours in resource libraries, phone calls to experts, and face-to-face visits.

Within my master's degree, much of the skills and theory I studied and practiced revolved around intercultural training, whether for high-school exchange students, study abroad students, or within more corporate settings. After two years in that educational space, I started my first U.S.-based position with Delphi International, an NGO that administered programs for the State Department's International Visitors Leadership Program. At that time, intercultural training was not integrated into such short-term programs and my focus turned to program development and logistics. It was in this work that I learned about the value of professional presentation and delivery, about the need to pay attention to every detail for a program to unfold smoothly. Both professional settings allowed me to expand my understanding of the broader field and develop different skill sets.

CHALLENGES INTERNATIONAL EDUCATION HAS FACED

Our field is no different from any other. The biggest challenge is also the biggest constant: that of change. The only way forward is to keep up with it, to embrace it, to process it, to learn from it, and to keep moving forward in the most inclusive and fairest ways possible. Perhaps the most important example is our current work to increase diversity and access to educational mobility programs, especially for those who identify with traditionally marginalized groups around race, gender, and economics.

Another area of significant change involves technology as it relates to the degree to which today's students are unable to disconnect from home and <u>be</u> in their host culture. When I studied abroad in 1982-1983, the practice was to spend a full academic year abroad, as semester programs were just starting to be offered and short-term, faculty-led programs were, well, they weren't. During my 10 months in Bogota, there was no expectation of personal contact with home beyond letters which usually took about 10 days to arrive. I knew that if there were an emergency, my family would reach me but other than two five-minute phone calls, I was completely focused on <u>being</u> in Colombia. I lived with a family, all but my Spanish language classes were in Colombian universities, and most of my friends were Colombian.

When I started teaching at SIT in 2005, we could still teach our graduate students to encourage their own students to leave technology behind. Perhaps a study abroad program might have a computer or two in the local office for students to access once a week or so. And to appease worried parents who wanted to know what was happening in a timely way, groups often selected a daily representative to post stories and photos online so that parents could see that their kids were OK. But only that one student was online each day so that the others could immerse themselves in their host communities more completely.

How would today's students react if they knew that they could not speak with their families and friends for months at a time once they left home? How would their parents? Would they even agree to such an experience? The ability to connect easily and cheaply with loved ones around the world means that today's sojourners are denied the opportunity to completely immerse themselves in their new cultures and communities. Even Peace Corps volunteers today connect with home in ways that were unheard of 20 or 30 years ago. The technology, the expectation of connection, is ubiquitous, really impossible to escape. As a result, as IE professionals, our job to encourage deep and meaningful engagement across difference is that much harder to facilitate. The challenge has shifted from "how to keep students off of their devices" to "how to promote learning in spite of and through students' devices."

While it is important to consider challenges that the field of international education has faced, it is also important to consider its successes. For example, the field has significantly professionalized, with peer-reviewed research that informs our practice, multiple opportunities for training and professional development, and a large global network for us to both work within and learn from. There is still so much work to do, but now we actively question assumptions that were held for decades, and we work conscientiously to bridge divides across identities, especially those related to including race, gender, and socio-economic status.

BEYOND 2023: WHERE WILL INTERNATIONAL EDUCATION GO?

I am often asked to share my thoughts about the future of international education as a field. As I've shared previously, I actually am not big on prognostication as the only thing we know for sure is that times will change, crises will happen, and change will be needed. We have learned that our field is always affected by the unknown. The 2001 attacks, the 2008 recession, the impacts of the #MeToo movement, the murder of George Floyd, and the pandemic... who could have predicted that these things would happen?

That said, professionals in our field are always ready for change, for shift. So while we don't yet know what it will be, we do know that it is likely that even five years from now, something will be different. We just don't know at this moment what it will be. What does this mean for us? Well, we need to have a variety of knowledge and skills ready to go, i.e., strong theoretical groundings, advocacy, management, professional writing, flexibility, knowledge of health/safety/security/crisis management, attention to detail, and even self-confidence, which research shows is a continued challenge for women especially.

I am very positive about the state of the field. Even as some leaders in our world fight for national or global domination, we are one world with 200 nations and thousands of cultures, and the need for people to live together will not go away. Yes, the field is fraught with challenge, including the lack of adequate financial resources for our students and our programs, continued issues for students and professionals who identify as members of minoritized groups, a huge focus on risk management/legalities/health and safety/regulations instead of on learning and connection across difference. With this in mind, it is ever more incumbent on IE professionals to always keep in mind why we do what we do, to both cherish and grow the joy we feel when learning and self-awareness happen, and to support those in the future who will consider our lived experiences as their histories. Doing so will help them to find their niches, make their impacts, and contribute to global peace and understanding. It may sound corny, but isn't that what international education is all about?

Author Bio

Sora H. Friedman, Ph.D., is a Professor of International and Global Education at SIT Graduate Institute. Her major research and practice interests include supporting rising professionals and women's leadership in international education. She has worked in the field of international education for 40 years, focusing on exchange program administration, public diplomacy, international training programs, and international policy advocacy. She joined the SIT Graduate Institute faculty full-time in 2005. At SIT, Sora supports new and career-transitioning IE professionals as they develop their skills and find their way into new professional opportunities. She teaches IE policy, theory, program design, research, and advocacy, and serves as Chair of SIT's Masters in IE degree programs. In addition to her work at SIT, Sora is a columnist with *GlobalEd* and sought-after speaker and trainer in the field. She is author of "How High the Ceiling: Gender and Leadership in International Higher Education" (in *The Wiley Handbook of Gender Equity in Higher Education*, 2021), co-author of

Careers in International Education: A Guide for New Professionals (with A. Reza, 2019), and currently is researching women's leadership in international education. Previously, Sora served in the Chair-streams of NAFSA's Teaching, Learning, and Scholarship Knowledge Community and Region XI, as well as national leadership positions including Chair of the Training Coordination Subcommittee and Trainer Corps. Sora holds a doctorate in cultural studies, an MA in international administration, a certificate in distance education, and a BA in politics and Spanish. She lived in England and Latin America, and is fluent in Spanish. Email: sora.friedman@sit.edu

About the Editors

THOMAS V. MILLINGTON is the Founder and Executive Director of Abroadia, a study abroad provider based in Geneva, New York. He was raised in a Bolivian-American household where he was first exposed to Latin American culture. He has over 20 years of experience in international education, beginning his career with Brethren Colleges Abroad (BCA), where he developed his philosophy of strengthening the connection between the field and issues of peace and justice and providing international opportunities for students from Tribal Colleges, HBCUs and HSIs. For a brief time, he served as Director of International Programs at Emmanuel College where he created a Program Approval Committee to review faculty-led program proposals while involving departments not traditionally associated with international education. At Emmanuel College, he encouraged faculty to develop and lead their own programs abroad. In 2009, he began to advocate for unemployed international educators and has researched this phenomenon extensively since then. He then accepted a position at Western Kentucky University as Director of Study Abroad and Global Learning. After leaving the university he assumed the position of resident director in Havana, Cuba for Spanish Studies Abroad. While there he established a homestay program, liaised with the Universidad de La Habana, and produced a "Resident Director's Manual". Since first visiting Cuba in 2002, he has become fascinated by the country and dedicated himself to promoting more engagement between American and Cuban universities. In 2013, he founded Abroadia and has since worked to create immersive study and volunteer opportunities for American students in Cuba and Latin America.

KRISHNA BISTA, Ed.D., is a Professor of Higher Education in the Department of Advanced Studies, Leadership and Policy at Morgan State University, Maryland, USA. Previously, Dr. Bista served as the Director of Global Education at the University of Louisiana at Monroe, where he was Chase Endowed Professor of Education in the School of Education. Dr. Bista is the founding chair of the Study Abroad and International Students (SAIS) SIG at the Comparative and International Education Society

(CIES). Recently, Dr. Bista completed his Fulbright Specialist tenure at the University of Southern Queensland, Australia. His recent books include *International Graduate and Doctoral Student Experience* (STAR Scholars, 2023), *Online Teaching and Learning in Asian Higher Education* (w/Cook & Saleh, Palgrave, 2023), *Reimagining Internationalization and International Initiatives at Historically Black Colleges and Universities* (w/Pinder, Palgrave, 2022), *Online Teaching and Learning in Higher Education During COVID-19* (w/Roy & Allen, Routledge, 2022); *International Students at US Community Colleges* (w/Malvaux, Routledge, 2021).

ROY Y. CHAN, Ph.D., is an Assistant Professor of Education and Ed.D. Program Director in Leadership and Professional Practice in the Helen DeVos College of Education at Lee University, Tennessee, USA. His research agenda broadly focuses on graduate and professional education, online and distance education, and international higher education. Dr. Chan served as Chair (2022-2023) of the Study Abroad and International Students (SAIS) SIG at the Comparative and International Education Society (CIES). He is the author of numerous books, including *Rethinking Hybrid and Remote Work in Higher Education: Global Perspectives, Policies, and Practices after COVID-19* (Palgrave Macmillan, 2023) and *Online Teaching and Learning in Higher Education During COVID-19: International Perspectives and Experiences* (Routledge, 2022).

BO ZHANG, Ed.D., is a TESOL instructor and district administrator at Providence Public Schools in Rhode Island who recently earned a doctoral degree in Educational Leadership at the University of Hartford in the U.S. Bo's research interests include international higher education, international student mobility, educational leadership, educational technology, and second language acquisition. The doctoral dissertation examined the experiences of international doctoral students while seeking employment in the United States. Bo co-edited *Crossing Borders, Bridging Cultures: The Narratives of Global Scholars* (2023), and currently fulfills various roles within the American Educational Research Association (AERA), TESOL International Association, NAFSA, STAR Scholars Network, New England Educational Research Organization (NEERO), and International Association of Student Affairs and Services (IASAS). Bo also serves as a reviewer for the Journal of Interdisciplinary Studies in Education and the Journal of Learning and Instruction.

Also Titles Supported by the Humane Letters Grant

Humane Letters Grant
KEEP FREE THINKING ALIVE

Made in the USA
Coppell, TX
04 November 2026

11207530R00062